KV-435-239

IEE TELECOMMUNICATIONS SERIES 8

SERIES EDITORS: PROFESSOR J.E. FLOOD AND C.J. HUGHES

Software design for electronic switching systems

Previous volumes in this series

Software design for electronic switching systems

S. TAKAMURA
H. KAWASHIMA
H. NAKAJIMA

Edited by
M.T. Hills

PETER PEREGRINUS LTD.
on behalf of the Institution of Electrical Engineers

Published by: The Institution of Electrical Engineers, London and New York
Peter Peregrinus Ltd., Stevenage, UK, and New York

English edition ©1979: Institution of Electrical Engineers

Originally published as 電子交換プログラム入門
©1976 Institute of Electronic and Communication Engineers of Japan

British Library Cataloguing in Publication Data

Takamura, S
    Software design for electronic swiching systems.
    - (Institution of Electrical Engineers. Tele-
    communications series).
    1. Telecommunication - Data processing
    2. Programming (Electronic computers)
    3. Telecommunication - Switching systems
    I.   Title II. Kawashima, H   III. Nakajima, H
    IV. Hills, Michael Turner   V. Series
    621.3815'37   TK5102.5

ISBN 0-906048-18-4

Composed at the Alden Press Oxford, London and Northampton
Printed in England by A. Wheaton & Co., Ltd., Exeter

621.3815'37
TAK

Foreword to the English edition

Among the most important technical innovations made in our times in the field of telecommunications is the recent development of electronic switching systems. It has opened a new possibility of providing an intelligent telecommunications network, which will meet the varying needs of modern societies in a flexible and economical manner, taking advantage of the fast-developing computer and electronic technologies. The development of electronic switching systems has many facets, one of the most important of which is no doubt that of an efficient and flexible software, not only for the online control of the switching systems, but also for the smooth and efficient running of offline software maintenance and administrative functions.

The present book, originally entitled 'Denshi Khokan Program Nyumon' (Introduction to the programming of electronic switching systems) published from the Institute of Electronics and Communication Engineers of Japan in March 1976, was produced, by Messrs. S. Takamura, H. Kawashima and H. Nakajima, as a result of the development work carried out in Japan since 1964. It describes the art of software design for electronic switching systems in a fairly comprehensive and detailed manner. It is a great pleasure for me to see that the book has been translated into English and thus presented in a more universal form, so that people not familiar with the Japanese language can read it.

The present translation is a product of marvellous international co-operation among those involved, both in the United Kingdom and in Japan. Among them, my special thanks go to Dr. M. T. Hills, who advocated initially that the translation would be a useful task and then devoted much time and effort to its editing by providing introductory and supplementary chapters, improving English wherever appropriate and editing some of the chapters.

All the goodwill and effort of those involved in the translation as well as the development work itself will be greatly rewarded if this English edition is widely read and makes some contribution, however small it may be, to the advancement of the art of software design for electronic switching systems, to be shared by interested people all over the world.

Dr. Bunichi Oguchi

Senior Managing Director and Chief Engineer, Nippon Telegraph and Telephone Public Corporation

Former Chairman of the Publishing Committee, The Institute of Electronics and Communication Engineers of Japan

7 December, 1978

Preface

Computer control of telephone and data-switching systems has now reached maturity as an established engineering endeavor. The software design for such systems uses many of the techniques of real-time programming developed in the online computing field but has also introduced a large number of its own techniques. These techniques are required to meet the special characteristics associated with electronic switching systems, the major characteristics of which include:

(*a*) complex functional specification

(*b*) need to interface to an enormous input/output subsystem with 10 000 or more terminals with response time requirements well below 1 s

(*c*) automatic provision of uninterrupted service in the presence of hardware and software faults and malfunctions

(*d*) need for a large number of sites each with individual variations

(*e*) complete support system to permit online modification and enhancement over a 20 or more years life

One example of a successful switching system is the Japanese D-10 family of systems which by 1978 had over 200 units in service. The Japanese have been credited with the pioneering of several software engineering techniques which can help satisfy the exacting requirements of modern switching systems. The more prominent example is their development of the state-transition diagram as an integral engineering tool for system specification and production.

The Japanese have always published English language articles on their techniques in their own publications and at International conferences. In 1976 the Institute of Electronic and Telecommunications Engineers of Japan published a book on the D-10 software entitled 'Programming electronic switching systems.' This book was intended for use only within Japan but it brought together a unified description of all the online and offline software components required in switching systems. This made it a unique publication and of interest to the whole of the electronic switching community rather than those interested only in the specific D-10 system. All the techniques described can be applied in one form or another to other switching systems. For this reason the book has been translated into English and supplemented with more recently published material. The resulting book has been edited to make it of interest to anybody involved in the production or procurement of electronic switching systems, as for the first time in book form a complete and detailed description has been provided of switching system software.

As a general background to the book, the editor has added a brief chapter describing the essential features of the Japanese telephone network together with an overview of the D-10 system.

After a general introduction to ESS programming the book first deals with the techniques used for online processing; the executive, call processing, input programs, analysis and translation and output programs. Next, it deals with the fault processing methods which maintain service in the presence of faults. The software requirements for the day-to-day administration of the system has a chapter.

The online portion is completed by a chapter describing how some specific services are programmed.

The latter part of the book deals with the offline support programs required to generate and maintain the online software. In particular, the techniques developed for system modularisation and management are described in the last chapter.

The level of treatment of the book assumes a basic knowledge of computers and programming techniques together with a knowledge of the requirements of a telephone switching system. The latter may be obtained, for instance, from 'Telecommunications switching principles' by M.T. Hills and published by Allen & Unwin and MIT Press in 1979.

The D-10 system was developed as a joint venture between the operating authority of the Nippon Telegraph and Telephone Public Corporation and the manufacturing companies of NEC, Hitachi, Oki Electronic Industries, and Fujitsu Ltd. This book has been possible by the work of engineers in all these organisations and in particular, by the authors of the original book, S. Takamura, H. Kawashima and H. Nakajima.

The costs of the translation were provided by the Japanese companies and the translation was mainly performed by Y. Shimizu (NEC), K. Wakizaka (Hitachi), K. Kondo (Oki) and K. Awaji (Fujitsu).

The editor is grateful to all these and many other unnamed participants for their efforts and, in particular, to Dr. B. Oguchi for his encouragement and support. He hopes that his editing has not performed any modification of their intent. He is grateful to the Institute of Electronic and Telecommunications Engineers of Japan for permission to use the material. The hope of everybody concerned in this project is that the result will be of assistance to those working in the field and maybe more importantly, those entering the field for the first time.

M.T. Hills
Virgina, USA
June 1979

Contents

Chapter 1

Introduction to the D-10

1.1 The Japanese telephone network

Public telecommunications within Japan are the sole responsibility of the Nippon Telegraph and Telephone Public Corporation (NTT). This is a body which was created in 1952, and took over from the Government the furnishing of telephone, telegraph and related telecommunication services. In Japanese, NTT is 'Nihon Denshin Denwa Kosha' and is usually referred to as 'Denden Kosha'.

International telecommunications are the responsibility of a private company called the Kokusai Denshin Denwa Co. Ltd., (KDD). This company was created in 1953 out of NTT.

The present Japanese telephone network has been created predominantly since 1945 and has many similarities to the North American System. In their publications on switching systems, the Japanese refer to the switching system by their North American names, in particular, *office*, for the local centre. In this book both office and local exchange are used interchangeably. Also the first stage in the trunk switching network is referred to as a *toll* exchange.

The network is arranged as a 4-level hierarchy. There are about 7000 *local exchanges* which are grouped into about 600 toll areas each served by *Toll Centre*. The toll centre areas are arranged into 79 groups each served by a *District Centre*. The top level of the hierarchy consists of 8 *Regional Centres*. These are nearly fully interconnected, but all are connected to the regional centres in Tokyo and in Osaka which can act as *National Centres* for switching between the remote district centres of Japan.

Multistage alternative routing is used from all levels of the hierarchy using conventional 'far-to-near' choice of routes. Four-wire switching is used for the District Centres, Regional Centres and almost all the toll centres.

Toll charging is performed at the toll centre for crossbar and step-by-step local exchanges. Periodic meter pulses are fed back to the local exchange by means of meter-pulse signals. The electronic systems perform their own charging for all national calls.

Switching machines in use

Functions of switching machine
The functions of a switching machine are classified as follows:

LS	Local (i.e. subscriber) switching
MS	Local tandem switch
TS	Toll switching
TTS	Toll transit switching

Thus district and regional centres must have the TTS function and these are now all 4-wire switched. The toll centres must have the TS functions and these are mostly 4-wire switched.

Until the introduction of D-10, the majority of the traffic was carried by crossbar.

Signalling systems
Between the subscriber and the local exchange normal 20 i.p.s. dial pulse signalling is standard but with an increasing number of m.f. pushbutton phones being installed on crossbar and electronic exchanges. The pushbutton phones conform to the CCITT standard.

Dial pulse signalling is used between step-by-step exchanges and between the earlier versions of smaller crossbar exchanges. The normal signalling though is m.f. (2 out of 5) on a link-by-link en-block basis (forward direction only). All crossbar systems can determine the correct number length by examining the initial one to four digits of the toll code. The district and regional centres can perform overlap receiving and sending of digital information. Separate channel signalling between electronic toll exchanges is installed in a number of cases.

A variety of line signalling systems are in use depending on the transmission media.

International calls
The international calls are handled by a separate company, KDD. They maintain the cable and satellite links with the rest of the world and also the gateway exchanges and international operator services. At the present time there is only limited subscriber dialling of outgoing calls.

To make an international call from Japan it is necessary to dial the KDD exchange and request the call. In an area served by D-10, a direct connection is possible, but outside this area it is necessary for the KDD to call the subscriber back. The charge for a call is accounted by KDD separately from a domestic call.

The introduction of the D-10 system is permitting international subscriber dialling, since these systems are capable of sending the calling line identity to the KDD equipment for the purposes of billing. The procedure for setting up an international call is to set up a path to the international exchange by the normal sequence of link-by-link signalling. Once the path is connected to the international exchange the calling number, a service required digit and the called numbers are transmitted end-to-end from the D-10 direct to the international exchange. The service required digit, dialled by the subscriber, indicates whether the call is

(*a*) fully automatic (access code '001').

(*b*) charge information required (access code '002'). This is provided automatically, once the call has finished the originating subscriber is called back and a synthesised message tells him the number dialled and the computed charge.

1.2 History of electronic switching development in Japan

What is now the D-10 project was started in 1964 when the Nippon Telegraph and Telephone Public Corporation (NTT) decided to establish a joint team with the four telephone equipment manufacturers of NEC, Hitachi, Oki Electric Industries and Fujitsu. The team was under the direction of the Electrical Communications Laboratories of the NTT.

Two projects were started, DEX-1 and DEX-T1, which were computer-controlled space and time-division speech networks, respectively. DEX stands for Dendenkosha Electronic Exchange. DEX-1 used duplicated, special-purpose computers for the control and an eight-stage network of 8×8 matrices for switching network, based on the Bell Laboratories ferreed switch. Also ferrods were used for line scanning. The DEX-T1 system was based on a central p.c.m. switch which served remote units consisting of (autonomous) analogue line concentrators which connected subscriber lines to a p.c.m. modem. DEX-1 was put into experimental service within the ECL Musashino Laboratory in 1965 and DEX-T1 in 1966.

These experiments showed that:

(a) Stored program control seemed promising for future development because of its unique merits, e.g. ability to add new service features, flexibility etc.

(b) Time division would not be economic for some time.

(c) Component reliability and operational stability was very good.

DEX-2

Accordingly, the decision was taken to proceed with the development of DEX-2 which was to be an economic competitor of standard C-400 crossbar. As well as economy, its design aims were for small volume and high reliability.

The speech-path network was chosen to be a 2-wire mechanically latching mini-crossbar switch on account of its small size, and no standing power requirement. Reed relays accessed by a diode matrix were used for the line scanner and the trunk circuits were given some elementary intelligence to minimise central processor load. To provide for separate development of speech network and processor, no special interface was built for the speech control equipment which had the same information format as the memory data bus.

The switching network was basically 8-stage using 8 × 8 matrices with a maximum capacity of 30 000 lines at 0·1 erlang per line.

The control of DEX-2 was designed based on the experience obtained from DEX-1. The new control was a 32-bit machine with duplicated central processors which would act as synchronised, separate or multiprocessor modes. The main temporary memories were 32K modules of 2·0 μs cycle time. Each memory could be addressed by either processor and sufficient modules were provided to give full duplication. Permanent memory modules of 64K capacity were provided by a metal card device. These too were duplicated. To reduce the cost of memory, two magnetic drums were also provided for subscriber data and non-real-time critical programs.

The processor was provided with a general purpose input-output channel to interface the drums and other standard peripheral devices. The order code provided for bit slice addressing of the memory and special macro instructions such as Search Unmatch Pattern used for the scanning and comparison operation.

A special feature of the design of the central processor complex was the introduction of computer-aided design for logic checking, part assignment and frame-wiring design. The actual part assignment was performed manually, but this was checked by the CAD program and automatic terminal allocation made. The frame-wiring program also checked noise margins and delay times. The software for DEX-1 was reminiscent of No. 1 ESS programming and was rather complicated. For DEX-2 the concept of the state-transition table was introduced, together with interpretive execution of the macro orders.

Two DEX-2 machines were built, one was installed in the Ushigome office in Tokyo and served initially 200 NTT head office subscribers, and later 3000 public subscribers. This system was cut into service in December 1969. The other system was installed at ECL Musashino Laboratories for program testing and other experiments.

DEX-21

Before the first DEX-2 was placed into service, it was clear that further economy was necessary and also that the new system should provide a wider range of functions such as toll switching, CENTREX, video switching, etc. It was also clear that the DEX-2 processor could usefully be made more general purpose so that it could be used for other applications, such as data switching etc. Finally, it was seen that a maximum size of 4000 erlangs (40 000 lines typically) would be preferable. For these reasons work started in 1968 on DEX-21 as a system with local, tandem, toll, CENTREX or video (and most combinations) functions.

To cater for the smaller exchanges, two further projects were started:

(i) DEX-R1 – a remote-control system using a DEX-21 system
(ii) DEX-A1 – an independent small-medium system.

The major changes from DEX-2 to DEX-21 were:

(*a*) The biggest change was to change the redundancy philosophy of fast memories, relay controllers and scanners to 'N + 1' rather than duplication.
(*b*) The drum memories were replaced by a high capacity drum with a 800 kW capacity.
(*c*) The margin design of logic and memory circuits was changed from worst case to a statistical design. This provided economisation and also allowed some speed-up of functions.
(*d*) The network was changed to provide concentration at both first and second stages of the line switch. This reduced the number of cross-points needed by 30%. The finger operation mechanism of the crossbar switch was improved to provide lower cost and weight. A 4-wire network was added for toll applications.
(*e*) The wired logic of the trunk circuits introduced design complications especially for 4-wire circuits. Hence 'pattern control' was used

by which the central processor operates and releases the relays directly as needed. Magnetically-latching relays were introduced into the trunk circuit.

(*f*) A miniature relay is used for the sensing element in the trunk circuit and a simplified reed-relay used for the line circuit.

The first DEX-21 office was put into service in December 1971 at Kasumigaseki Office in Tokyo, where it offers CENTREX service to 2000 telephones of NTTs head office.

Commercial system D-10
Based on the success of the DEX-21 models the system was adopted by the NTT. The commercial name of the system is D-10 and the standard system has further economisations compared to DEX-21 primarily on equipment mounting to reduce its volume even further.

1.3 The D-10 system

1.3.1 D-10 outline
The D-10 system family may be used for the complete range of switching functions in a national telephone network. This includes local exchanges of up to 100 000 lines with various tandem functions and the full range of trunk exchanges (2- and 4-wire) with sizes up to 8192 incoming and 8192 outgoing. In addition, such features as CENTREX and videophone are used. The range of signalling systems include not only all the existing register and trunk signalling but also the newly introduced common channel signalling system.

The basic hardware configuration shown in Fig. 1.1 is divided into a speech path subsystem, a central processor subsystem and an I/O (input/output) subsystem.

1.3.2 Speech path subsystem
The speech path (SP) subsystem consists of the switching network, trunks circuits together with the driver and scanner circuits to interface into the central processor. The switching network is constructed from a mechanically-latched 8 × 8 mini crossbar switch. The switch is operated by 10 ms pulses and therefore dissipates significantly less heat than the conventional electrically-latched crossbar switch. The switch also has a much shorter operate and release time than the conventional crossbar switch. In the local exchange, the speech path network consists of up to 16 each of two subnetworks:

(a) *Line link network (LLN):* A four-stage link network which can connect from 2048 up to 12 288 subscribers lines onto 1024 internal junctors. This is a two-wire switch, no holding or test wire is required as the switch is mechanically latched and as the processor maintains a map in its memory of the state of a switch.

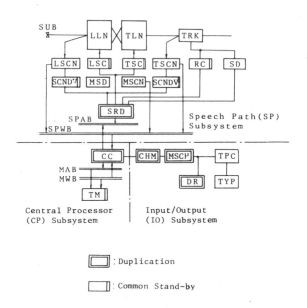

LLN	:Line link network	TSC	:TLN switch controller
TLN	:Trunk link network	RC	:Relay controller
TRK	:Trunk equipment	SPAB	:Speech path address bus
LSCN	:Line scanner	SPWB	:Speech path answer bus
TSCN	:Trunk scanner	CC	:Central control
SRD	:Signal receiver distributor	TM	:Temporary memory
MSD	:Maintenance signal distributor	CHM	:Channel multiplexer
MSCN	:Maintenance scanner	MSCH	:Multiplex subchannel
SCR	:Switch controller register	DR	:Magnetic drum
SCNDV	:Scanner driver	TPC	:Teletypewriter papertape
SD	:Signal distributor		reader controller
LSC	:LLN switch controller	TYP	:Teletypewriter

Fig. 1.1 *Hardware configuration*

(b) *Trunk link network (TLN):* A four-stage network which connects 1024 internal junctors onto 1024 output terminations. These output terminations include incoming and outgoing trunk circuits, signalling receivers and senders, and service circuits such as ringing current generators. For local switch applications this is a two-wire switch and for trunk switching applications a four-wire switch is used.

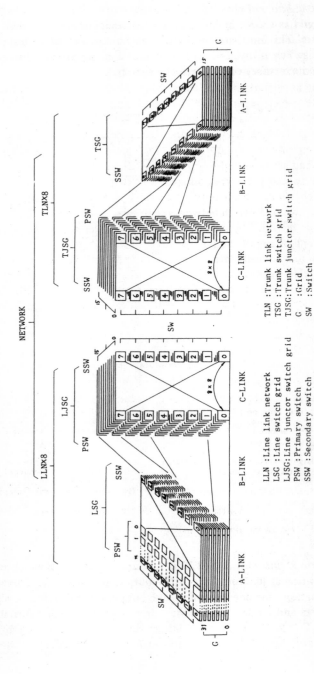

LLN :Line link network
LSG :Line switch grid
LJSG:Line junctor switch grid
PSW :Primary switch
SSW :Secondary switch

TLN :Trunk link network
TSG :Trunk switch grid
TJSG:Trunk junctor switch grid
G   :Grid
SW :Switch

Fig. 1.2   *Network configuration*

The logical and physical building block of the link networks is a two-stage grid as shown in Fig. 1.2. The first-stage grids are shown as horizontal planes and the second-stage grids are shown as vertical planes in Fig. 1.2. Physically, one stage of a grid consists of two plug-in boards which can be inserted and removed with ease.

Line and trunk circuits are provided to detect calling conditions and provide speech supervision. The line circuit consists of a reed relay for call detectors and a cutoff relay which is mounted directly on the line switch grid which is incorporated in the first stage crossbar switch. The trunk circuits are based on the use of one or two magnetically-latching relays and are mounted four trunk circuits to a plug-in board.

The speech paths are controlled by switch controllers, one provided for each trunk switch networks (trunk switch controller − TSC) and one for two line switch networks (line switch controller − LSC). Redundancy is provided by one spare switch controller which can be switched in to replace any of the LSC or TSC.

The magnetically-latching relays in the trunk circuits are controlled by a relay controller (RC). Relays which require accurate timing or rapid operation are controlled by a signal distributor (SD). The relay controller consists of a relay tree which can only operate or release one relay at a time. This is less expensive than the signal distributor which permits the direct operation or release of a relay.

The state of the subscriber lines is determined by a line scanner (LSCN) provided one per 4096 lines. The trunk line states are determined by a trunk scanner provided one per 1024 trunks.

Orders of speech path operations and requests for scanning information are received from the processor subsystem by the signal receiver and distributor (SRD). This decodes the address and distributes the appropriate command to the required scanner or driver. The SRD is fully duplicated.

Diagnostic information about the speech path subsystem is collected by a maintenance scanner (MSCN). Reconfigurations of the various drivers or parts of the scanner is achieved by a maintenance signal distributor (MSD).

Scan point addressing circuits are mounted as part of the line switch frame and trunk circuits frame. The remainder of the speech path control equipment is mounted on a speech path control frame (SPCF).

A summary of the speech path subsystem is given in Table 1.1.

1.3.3 Central processor (CP) subsystem
The D-10 system is under the control of a 32-bit processor. The central control (CC) of the processor is duplicated and provides 130

Table 1.1 *Speech path equipment*.

Abbreviation code	Equipment name	General description	Main parts	Maximum number of equipment
LLN	Line link network	Four stage switching network, comprising 8 × 8 matrix switch for each stage, accommodates 2084 ~ 12 288 lines and 1024 junctors	Small crossbar switch, small relay, reed relay	LLN + TLN = 16
TLN	Trunk link network	Nearly the same configuration as LLN, accommodates 1024 trunk terminals and 1024 junctors, 2-wire switching for LS and 4-wire switching for TS	Small crossbar switch, small relay	
TRK	Trunk circuits	Trunk circuits, mounted on a jack-in type package, controlled by the relay controller (RC) according to instructions from central control	Magnetic latch relay	
LSCN	Line scanner	Scanner for detecting call originations, comprising 32 rows × 128 columns array (4096 points)	Electronic circuits	20
TSCN	Trunk scanner	Scanner for discriminating status of trunks, comprising 32 rows × 64 columns array (2048 points)	Electronic circuits	16
SRD	Signal receiver and distributor	Common part of speech path controllers, information interface station to and from CC, duplicated	Electronic circuits	2 × 2
MSD	Maintenance signal distributor	Signal distributor for test, diagnosis and changeover signals to speech path equipment	Electronic circuits	2

Table 1.1   *contd.,*

Abbreviation code	Equipment name	General description	Main parts	Maximum number of equipment
MSCN	Maintenance scanner	Scanner for discriminating status of speech path control equipment	Electronic circuits	2 × 2
LSC	Line link speech path controller	Controller for LLN switches, 1 LCS controls 2 LLN	Electronic circuits	6
TSC	Trunk link speech path controller	Controller for TLN switches, 1 TSC controls 1 TLN	Electronic circuits	16
SD	Signal distributor	High-speed signal distributor, which controls timing precise relays (e.g. DP, MF sender relays), comprising 16 rows × 16 columns array	Electronic circuits	2 (basic)
RC	Relay controller	Low speed signal distributor, which controls TRK magnetic latch relays, comprising 32 rows × 64 columns array	Electronic circuits	12, 2 (standby)

Table 1.2   *Central processor and I/O subsystem equipment*

Abbreviation code	Equipment name	General description	Main parts	Maximum number of equipment
CC	Central control	Decode program instructions, perform specified operations and control entire system. Organised on a word basis, with a word length of 32 bits, have 119 basic instructions and 12 optional instructions. Can be operational in dual multiprocessor mode.	Electronic circuits	1 × 2
TM	Temporary memory	Store programs and data required in switching operations and also store drum resident programs transiently. Capacity: 32 kilowords × (32 + 1) bit. Cycle time: 1·44 μs.	Ferrite core, electronic circuits	8
CHM	Channel multiplexor	Common part of data channels, which control data transfer among I/O devices and TMs. 1 CHM controls 4 MSCH. Duplicated.	Electronic circuits	1 × 2
MSCH	Multiplex subchannel	Individual part of data channels. 1 MSCH controls 8 IOC (Input output controller) by time division multiplexing.	Electronic circuits	8
DRU	Magnetic drum unit	Store subscriber data and nonurgent programs, also used for back-up memory against TM failure. Duplicated. Capacity: 870 kilowords (= 1024 words × 848). Rotation speed: 3000 turn per minute. Average access time: 10 ms.	Floating head drum, electronic circuits	1 × 2 (standard office)

Table 1.2 *contd.,*

Abbreviation code	Equipment name	General description	Main parts	Maximum number of equipment
DRC	Magnetic drum controller	Controller of DRU. 1 DRC controls 8 DRU, but in the standard office. 1 DRC controls 1 DRU.	Electronic circuits	1×2 (standard office)
TYP	Teletypewriter	Input of operation and maintenance commands, output of system status. Paper tape punch is also available. Input/output speed: 600 characters per minute.	Mechanical parts	3
PTR	Paper-tape reader	Input of large amount of data and commands. Phototransistor type. Input speed: 120 characters per second.	Mechanical parts	1
TPC	TYP and PTR controller	Control TYP and PTR	Electronic circuits	1×2

instructions. The main memory of the processor consists of 32K word temporary memory (TM) units which are connected to the central control by a memory bus which can accommodate up to 8 TM units.

One of the distinguishing features of the D-10 system is the use of an 800K word magnetic drum (DR) which is used for secondary and back-up storage. This drum and the other input/output equipment such as magnetic type units and teletypewriters communicate with the central control via a data channel (DCH) which permits the central control to perform other jobs in parallel with the information transfer. Information transfer between the central control, speech path subsystems and temporary memory is performed by buses. Buses consist of an *n*-pair cable and are of two types:

(i) A.C. (alternating current) bus which is virtually noise-proof since all equipment connects to the bus via transformers.

(ii) D.C. (direct current) bus used for central control to temporary memory only because of its faster speed.

The redundancy philosophy of the processor subsystem is to duplicate the main equipment such as the central control but to provide temporary memory units on an $n + 1$ basis. This is described in more detail in Chapter 8.

Table 1.2 summarises the characteristics of the processor subsystem.

1.3.4 Software organisation

The basic software consists of five parts:

(i) Executive control program (EP) — which controls the execution of the other programs.

(ii) Fault processing program (FP) — which recognises the existence of an abnormal situation in the system and then attempts to restore the system to operational status by appropriate reconfigurations.

(iii) Diagnostic program (DP) — which locates the faulty device within a subsystem switched out of service.

These three parts are basically the same for any type of exchange (i.e. local, trunk etc.) and for any particular exchange. The remaining two parts contain specific parts relating to the type of exchange and to the detailed functions provided in particular exchanges.

(iv) Call processing program (CP)

(v) Administration program (AP) — which deals with technician requests from the teletypewriter for change of system information (such as subscriber's telephone number, class of service etc.) and which provide the traffic and other operating statistics.

In addition, there is test program software provided for automatically testing the system during installation and after repairs.

Finally, there is the support software which maintains and produces the individual files for loading into particular D-10 systems.

1.4 Summary of the main D-10 characteristics

1.4.1 Hardware

(i) Whilst the trunking scheme differs for different applications, the basic hardware configuration is the same.

(ii) There is independence between the speech path subsystems and the central control subsystem. This permits independent evolution of the two parts. There is a standardised interface to the computer peripherals.

(iii) The use of a high-capacity magnetic drum providing significant economy in storage.

(iv) The $N + 1$ redundancy system as applied to temporary memory units as well as speech path controllers. This system has been proved to work very satisfactorily (Chapter 8).

(v) The use of a miniature crossbar switch and miniature magnetically latching relays to realise miniaturisation.

1.4.2 Software

(i) Standardisation of the software so that a particular application may be obtained by selection and edition of the necessary program modules from a master file (Chapter 13).

(ii) Complete separation of the exchange dependent information such as the trunking scheme and number of circuits (Chapters 9 and 11).

(iii) The introduction of the state-transition diagram for the functional description of the program (Chapter 3).

(iv) The introduction of interpretive execution to achieve economy and simpler adaptability (Chapter 7).

Chapter 2

Introduction to ESS programming

2.1 Characteristics of switching programs

An ESS is under the control of a single processor (or relatively few processors) but it must be capable of dealing with very large numbers of simultaneous calls. The processor must therefore be organised as a multiprocessor so that each telephone call appears to have its own processor. The time-sharing techniques developed for conventional real-time computers used for scientific or business applications have little relevance to the requirements of ESSs.

An ESS has to deal with tens of thousands of input lines and process several thousand calls in parallel. Typically a call lasts between 100 to 200s but within this time, the processor is required only to effect a few switching operations when a speech path is connected or released. The remaining time is devoted to what is called supervision which is looking for signalling conditions indicating requests to change the state of a connection. Supervision is associated with traffic-carrying hardware units and is achieved by executing a process at periodic intervals to scan the hardware looking for changes. Once a valid change is detected, it must be processed to determine its meaning and the appropriate output commands issued to the speech path subsystem to modify the connection pattern or to transfer signalling information to another exchange. This type of multiprocessing requires the following characteristics:

(i) *Execution sequence control (executive):* The execution-sequence-control mechanism is used to schedule the processor time for its various tasks. This is the function often called the executive in conventional real-time systems. For ESS applications the operation of the executive has to be very efficient.

(ii) *Resource managment:* Large numbers of calls have to be processed simultaneously and this implies that there will be many demands for common resources within the system such as memory blocks and input/output equipment. The amount of these resources is decided in advance based on the traffic estimates for the system. A centralised resource management system is necessary to ensure effective utilisation of these shared resources.

(iii) *Traffic load control:* Calls arrive at random and an unexpected high level of traffic may cause a resource shortage. This results in a temporary worsening of the grade of service. Worse still, the overload may have a disruptive effect upon the ESS and this can severely affect surrounding exchanges. To avoid these situations it is necessary to build into the system the capability to continually monitor the incoming traffic and restrict the traffic when an exceptionally high level occurs to prevent the overload disrupting the system.

(iv) *Service continuity:* A general-purpose computer ordinarily stops its operation for periodic maintenance checks. However, an ESS must provide continuous service even in the presence of faults in the hardware or software. Protection against hardware faults require fault detection circuits plus the capability to switch in spare controllers.

Software faults are caused by hardware faults or undetected program bugs. An example of a software fault is if the map within the processor memory of the speech path network ceases to mirror the actual state of the network. When a software fault is detected it is necessary to instigate a restart process program to restore the stored data to normal. The restart process consists of a series of levels of increasing severity to the calls in progress. The most severe restart process is one which clears all calls in progress and resets all hardware and data areas to a known null state. In general, the effect of minor software faults can be corrected with less disruption on the system.

(v) *Program maintainability:* One of the principal objectives of the introduction of SPC into switching systems is to enable the expansion of facilities without modification of the hardware and also the development of hardware without modification of the functions. Also the whole system is designed for a long life and therefore the maintainability of the software is exceedingly important. Techniques used to achieve these objectives include:

(*a*) Choice of a software structure which facilitates functional addition or change

(*b*) Capability for hardware expansion and software replacement whilst the system remains operational

(*c*) Development of support software for system maintenance (*d*) Development of software engineering techniques which limit the volume of programs to be maintained

(*e*) Provision of documentation which is easily understandable.

2.2 ESS program organisation

Programs for ESSs fall into two categories, the *online* program which operates the actual exchange and the *offline* program which runs on some other computer to generate the online program and its required data for a particular exchange. In addition a special online program called the construction program is required for testing the system as it is being assembled.

Fig. 2.1 shows the general arrangement of the operational online program. As explained earlier this consists of five parts.

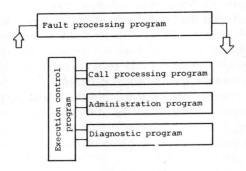

Fig. 2.1   *Switching program configuration*

(i) *Execution control program:* This program provides the time-sharing required to make the system multiprocessing. It performs the following functions:

(*a*) activation of a series of processes in a preset list of priorities

(*b*) provision for data transfer between processes and input/output devices

(*c*) manage memory and input/output resources

(*d*) provide basic sense of time for the system

(ii) *Call processing program:* This is the program which directly controls the switching operation of the various calls originating from the telephones or trunk lines. The program has two parts, one which determines the switching requirements and the other which executes the required operation.

(iii) *Administrative program:* This program provides the functions required to administer the system. This includes the features:

(*a*) monitoring the grade of service given to different classes of subscribers and trunk lines and providing the means to modify the grade of service if necessary

(*b*) modification of the data stored for particular subscribers or trunk lines. This includes directory number, features etc.

(*c*) adding and modifying subscribers and trunk lines

(*d*) modification of traffic recording and processing functions

(*e*) initiation of test functions for preventive maintenance and checking of repairs.

The administrative programs are executed when required by the maintenance personnel.

(iv) *Fault processing program:* Good switching service is provided when the above programs work normally. Whenever a fault is detected the fault processing program must be called automatically. This progam then recognises the source of the fault and if necessary causes the switch over to standby units followed by suitable restart of the system. The main objective is to minimise the time taken to restore normal service and to minimise the disruption noticed by the subscribers.

(v) *Diagnostic program:* The fault processing program merely locates a fault to a unit which can be switched out of service. The function of the diagnostic program is to isolate the cause of the fault so that it may be repaired. The diagnostic program can be activated automatically or by command from maintenance personnel. It consists of a large number of test programs which print the test results into a teletypewriter. The maintenance personnel use a previously prepared table called a diagnostic dictionary which relates the different test results to particular plug-in *cards* which may be the cause of a fault.

Fig. 2.2 shows the general relationship between these five program classes.

In the D-10, the offline support software has been written to run on an extended version of the D-10 processor. The specially extended processors are located in a small number of 'software centres' around the country. These processors are under the control of an operating

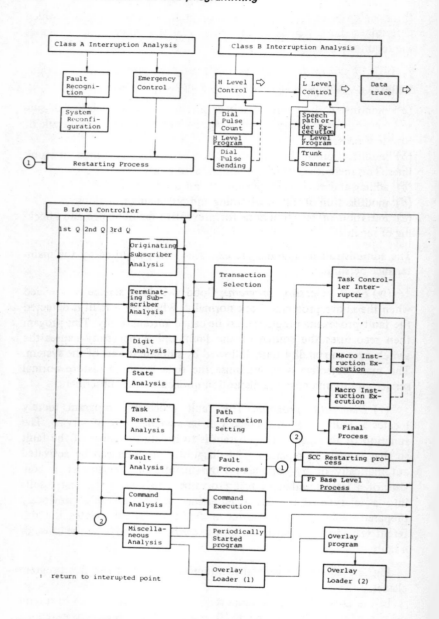

Fig. 2.2 *Program configuration (flow of control sequence)*

system which controls the flow of work through the system and activates the various jobs required to produce the online programs. The jobs required include:

(*a*) *Language processors* to convert into machine language a program written in assembly language (or one of the specialised languages to be discussed later)

(*b*) *Office data generation* this program takes the detailed specification of the office configuration and generates the data for the online program.

(*c*) *Office data regenerator* once a system is placed into service there will be many day to day changes to the stored data base entered directly from a teletypewriter on the online machines. Whenever a major extension or modification of a system is required, it is necessary to take a copy of the stored data base and regenerate the data as it would have appeared on an original office specification. The new data may now be merged with the regenerated data and a new data prepared.

The functions of the software centre are covered in detail in Chapter 12.

Chapter 3

The executive

3.1 Introduction

The switching program system is made up of a number of programs each of which has a definite function. Whenever the processor gives control to one of these programs it is said to perform a task. The main function of the executive program is to schedule the performance of the many tasks required to process a telephone call and to control the central resources required by the tasks.

Tasks differ from each other in regard to their real-time requirements. The tolerance for the accuracy on the time of activation of a particular task varies from a minimum of a few milliseconds to a maximum of several seconds. Generally, input-output tasks have the most severe real-time requirement. Of these the dial pulse counting task has the most severe real-time characteristic and even a few milliseconds delay in its activation can result in directing a call to a wrong number. On the other hand, a fairly long time delay may be allowed for tasks as 'digit analysis', 'digit translation', 'call status analysis' etc., because a second or so delay will never give an incorrect treatment of the call apart from a slight increase in the total call connection time.

The D-10 system must provide a time-sharing structure to activate the tasks within the different tolerances required. In this structure, the programs are allocated to one of several groups of 'execution levels . These execution levels are ordered from high to low level. A program used for a high-urgency task is allocated to a high-execution level group. Apart from those programs which are in the highest level, no program is allowed to continuously occupy the central control. A task is forced to be interrupted whenever a higher-level task occurs and the lower-level task must wait until the higher-level program completes its task. That is, lower-level programs can occupy the central control only in the intervals when higher-level programs do not require the central control. This mechanism is controlled by a special hardware system called the interrupt system in co-operation with software described below.

This time-sharing program structure makes it possible for various programs to effectively use the central control in parallel to perform tasks without any undue effect on the real-time requirements of each task.

3.2 Interrupt system

The basis of the interrupt system is a number of registers called 'interrupt source flip-flops' (ISF) which are provided corresponding to individual 'interrupt signals' (IS). The interrupt signals are produced by various circuits both inside and outside of the central control, such as a millisecond clock circuit, trouble detection circuits, data channel equipment etc., and sometimes caused by manual operation. Each of these interrupt source flip-flops is assigned an interrupt priority called interrupt level.

When one of the interrupt source flip-flops receives an interrupt signal, the interrupt mechanism causes the central control to stop the current task, store the program address at which it was interrupted, and transfer the control to an appropriate interrupt source analysis program. The interrupt source analysis program analyses the interrupt source and transfers the control to the corresponding 'task program'. When this task program is completed, the control is returned to the interrupted program. An interrupt source assigned to a particular level can only interrupt programs of lower interrupt level.

Fig. 3.1 illustrates the overall scheme in the interrupt-level hierarchy in the D-10 system. The levels are divided into three major groups. From the highest to the lowest, these are:

(i) *Fault interrupt levels* which are initiated by various trouble detection circuits. These contain programs which activate the various fault processing programs to recognise the source of a trouble, isolate the faulty devices and restore the system to a normal state.

(ii) *Clock interrupt levels* which are activated by the millisecond clock circuit every 4 ms. Almost all the input-output programs are included in this level.

(iii) *Base level* where programs are activated in a different manner from the above two cases, because the base level tasks are not associated with any interrupt (the details are shown below). All deferrable programs are included in this level and are called *base level programs*.

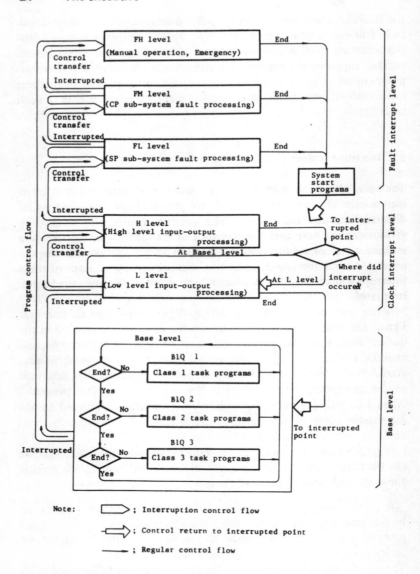

Fig. 3.1   *Interrupt level configuration and control flow*

Fig. 3.1 shows that the fault levels are subdivided into three levels, i.e. the fault-high, -middle and -lower levels (FH, FM and FL levels) programs are assigned to one of the levels depending upon the degree of urgency required in fault processing. In other words, to the degree to which a fault will affect the whole system. Thus, faults concerned with the central processor subsystem are placed in the FM level, while almost all faults in the speech path system are considered to be local faults, so are placed to the lowest FL level. The FH level is an exceptional level used for a system initialisation or debugging.

The clock level is also subdivided into two levels, high and low (H and L) according to the real-time requirement of each of the clock level tasks. For example, a program for dial pulse counting or sending is placed in the H level and a program for network and trunk operations is placed in the L level.

Though the base level includes programs with less real-time characteristics, it is also subdivided into three preference levels, from the highest to the lowest, B1Q1, B1Q2 and B1Q3. As mentioned before, a wider time tolerance may be allowed for all base level programs to perform their tasks, but there are still some differences in the tolerances between say, call processing programs and administrative programs. This is especially true when the system becomes overloaded by heavy traffic. Thus, call processing programs are generally placed at the B1Q1 or B1Q2 level and administrative programs, some routine test programs, diagnostic programs and so on are placed at the lowest, B1Q3, level.

3.3 Program control flow

Fig. 3.1 also shows the general program control flow between the various interrupt levels. Interrupts caused by device faults and manual operation are generally called class A interrupts. When one of these interrupts occurs, control is transferred to the Class A interrupt source analysis (AISANL) program. The AISANL program analyses the interrupt source, identifies the fault and activates the corresponding fault processing program. This is normally followed by an appropriate restart program, before the control is returned to the interrupted programs (see Chapter 8).

The 4 ms clock interruption is called a class B interrupt together with interrupts from I/O devices. The Class B interrupt source analysis (BISANL) program, works in a very similar manner to the AISANL program. When a clock interrupt occurs, the BISANL first transfers control to the H level control (HLCTL) program. The HLCTL program has a *program activation control timetable* in which the various H level programs are scheduled to perform tasks at appropriate intervals of 4 ms multiples. The HLCTL program activates each of the programs that are scheduled to run at the present interrupt cycle. When it completes all these tasks the HLCTL transfers the control to the low level control (LLCTL) program. If the clock interrupt had occurred whilst L level tasks were still running, HLCTL returns control to those interrupted tasks rather than LLCTL. (This is described in more detail in the next Section).

The LLCTL program also has its own timetables and acts in a very similar manner to the HLCTL program. After completion of all programs, the HLCTL program returns the control to whatever base level program had been running when the clock interrupt occurred.

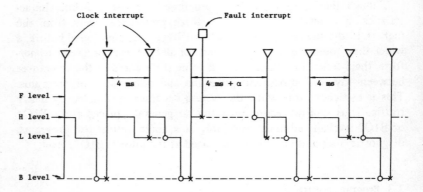

Fig. 3.2   *Interruption level diagram*
    x   Interruption
    o   Restart from interrupted point
    ---- Interrupted state

Fig. 3.2 shows the control flow in a level diagram. As shown in the Figure, the H level regularly completes tasks within 4 ms every cycle, unless it happens to be interrupted by some fault level tasks. On the other hand, the L level is occasionally interrupted by the H level before it completes the tasks and, as a result, some tasks remain uncompleted until the next cycle. That is, the L level tasks are occasionally forced to skip some interrupt cycles and, as a result, their execution plan will sometimes deviate from the original plan. This is the reason why only those tasks which required a very severe real time characteristic are assigned to the H level. Other tasks which will be only marginally affected by some delay in execution time are assigned to the L level.

3.4 Program activation control by timetables

The tasks required for a switching system are classified into two groups with apparently different characteristics, *supervision* tasks and *processing* tasks. Supervision tasks detect input signals caused inside or outside the system. Processing tasks process these inputs and output appropriate data for operating the peripheral equipment. Programs which are responsible both for the supervision tasks and for the peripheral operating tasks are called input-output programs.

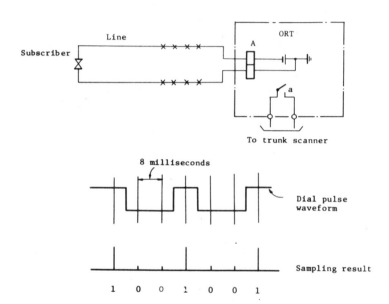

Fig. 3.3 *Dial pulse counting*

These input-output programs work in a specific manner, in which they are activated at suitable intervals. They are called *cyclic programs*. For example, Fig. 3.3 illustrates the operation of the dial pulse counting task. The loop condition of a subscriber's line is registered by a relay in the originating register trunk circuit. This condition is available at a scan point. The dial pulse count program is activated at 8 ms intervals and reads the sense point in the originating register trunk via the trunk scanner and therefore samples the dial pulse waveform which enables it to count dial pulses.

The organisation of the control tables for the high level control program is shown in fig. 3.4. The starting addresses of each of the H level

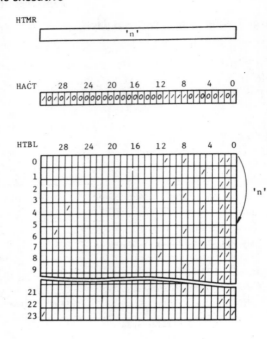

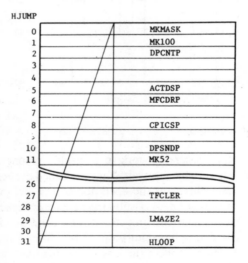

Fig. 3.4   *Program activation control tables and words*

cyclic programs is contained in the HJUMP table. This consists of 32 consecutive words. For instance, the 3rd word contains the starting address for the digit pulse count program.

The activation pattern for these programs is set out as a timetable in the HTBL table. This table consists of 24 consecutive words, each of which is associated with a particular 4 ms interval within a 96 ms cycle. Within each of 0 to 23 words, bits 0 to 31 are associated with the cyclic programs whose starting address are stored in the corresponding words 0 to 31 in the HJUMP table. Thus, each column of the timetable is associated with a cyclic program. Each column has an activity bit in the corresponding bit position in the HACT word. If the activity bit of a column is equal to 1, the 1s marked within the column designate the 4 ms intervals during which the associated program is due for execution. The timetable shows that the MK100 program is activated on all 4 ms intervals and the DPCNTP program is activated on odd 4 ms intervals. The HLOOP programs is activated only once every 96 ms.

The function of the HACT word is to activate or deactivate particular tasks. This facility is used during periods of overload when certain scanning functions may be suspended until the overload has cleared.

The count indicating the current 4 ms interval is stored in the HTMR word. This is used as a pointer to select one of the 24 timetable rows. The count is incremented by one one each millisecond clock interrupt and is reset to zero once every 96 ms.

When a clock interrupt occurs, the H level control program works as follows:

(*a*) It first reads the interval count in the HTMR word. The count shows either 0 through 23.

(*b*) It reads one of the 24 words in the HTBL table, to which the interval count points.

(*c*) If the count is 23 it is reset to 0 otherwise it increments the interval count and stores it in the HTMR.

(*d*) The selected timetable word is 'ANDed' with the HACT word. The ANDed word contains a 1 in every bit position in which both the timetable word and the HACT word contain a 1. Thus, each position marked by a 1 designates a program that is ready and due for execution in the present clock interval.

(*e*) It finds a 'rightmost' bit position marked by a 1 in the ANDed word.

(*f*) If it finds a 1, it indexes the HJUMP table with the number of the bit position where a 1 is found, and obtains the starting address of a cyclic program. Then it unconditionally transfers the control to the cyclic program.

(*g*) When the cyclic program is completed, a transfer is made back to step (*e*), where the HLCTL program searches for a 'next rightmost' 1 this time.

(*h*) It recycles the steps (*e*), (*f*) and (*g*) until it finds no more 1s in the ANDed word.

(*i*) It transfers the control to the L level control program or the interrupted program, as mentioned before.

In a switching system, a number of tasks have to be performed on a cyclic basis with a wide range of intervals and priorities. Accordingly, the D-10 system provides a total of seven kinds of timetables, i.e. one timetable for the H level programs, two timetables for the L level programs and four timetables for the base level programs. They are very similar to each other in the table scheme and the accompanying control data, but the intervals and cycles vary from a minimum of 4 ms interval and 96 ms cycle to a maximum of one hour interval and 24 hour cycle, depending on the purposes.

3.5 Program activation control with queues

The previous Section outlined one of two different activation control methods, in which programs are cyclically activated at selected intervals according to program activation control timetables. The other method, which is used for all base level programs, is shown in Fig. 3.5. Input programs, when they detect a signal from a peripheral equipment, store the signal plus other identifying information into a transaction memory block called a *hopper*. This hopper is then attached to either one of three queues, i.e. 1st Q, 2nd Q and 3rd Q, according to a priority given to each of requests.

When the base level control program (BLCTL) obtains control, it examines a queue to see if there is any work. If it finds a request, it detaches the hopper from the queue and transfers the control to a specific base level program which is responsible for processing the request. In this processing, the BLCTL program is subject to a specific rule called a *ceiling control*, in which, as shown in the Figure, each time when the BLCTL program completes all requests in a specific queue, a program switch called 'ceiling control switch' steps to a next point, so that the BLCTL program can find requests in the next lower priority queue. The switch is initialised to point to the 1st Q each time the program control returns from clock level to base level. This mechanism prevents the activation control from examining empty queues in vain, because once a queue becomes empty, it is likely to remain so until the next execution of clock level programs, by which most of the inputs are detected.

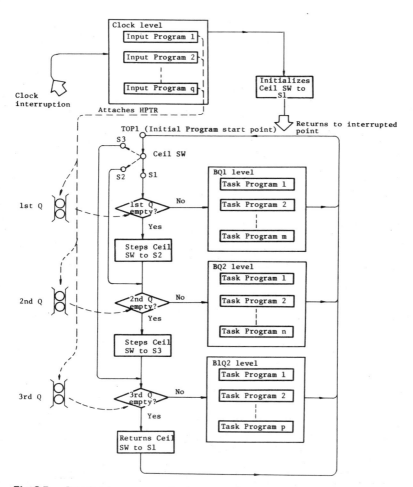

Fig. 3.5 *Base level program activation control*

Thus, the base level control program makes it possible to service higher-priority requests in preference to lower priority ones regardless of the time when they have been attached.

Figure 3.6 shows how transaction memory blocks are chained in a queue. The HEADP word holds an address data to point the head block in the queue and, similarly, the TAILP word holds an address data to point the tail block in a chain. All blocks in the chain also have an address data in the 2nd word to point the next block, except that the last block contains 0 to show itself being the last in the chain.

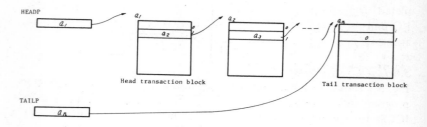

Fig. 3.6   *Transaction block queue*

An operation to attach or detach a block to or from a queue is very simple. Generally, a 'new' block is attached to the tail of the queue and an 'old' block is detached from the head in the queue. For instance, a block is attached by storing the new block head address into both the TAILP word and the 2nd word of the last block, and the head block in the chain is detached only by changing the contents of the HEADP word to point the 2nd block. The chain scheme illustrated above is called in a term of a 'first-in-first-out' (FIFO) since each block in the chain is sequentially detached according to the order when it was attached.

3.6 Input/output units control program

Generally, input/output (I/O) units are extremely slow in their operation speed as compared with a central control. Therefore, it is very inefficient for a central control to be fully engaged in controlling I/O units all the while it reads or writes data from, or to, I/O units. This problem is avoided by the use of the data channel equipment. A data channel equipment, once instructed by a central control, acts for the central control to read or write the data and interrupts the central control once it has completed the required operation.

A switching program system includes many programs which need to use I/O units. From the point of view of program design and management it is uneconomical to have individual programs provided with the complicated input/output sections. The D-10 system provides a special group of programs called 'input/output control program system' (IOCS) as an access program to I/O units, through which any program can easily access to any of I/O units. User programs which require access to one of I/O units, have only to call the corresponding IOCS as a subroutine. The IOCS waits while the necessary I/O operation is completed. Thus, the IOCSs make it possible to manage the commonly used I/O units in a single modular program for easy program design and management.

3.6.1 IOCS structure

Fig. 3.7 shows an IOCS functional block diagram, in relation to a user program and a hardware. This Figure shows a common structure to all IOCSs for various I/O units, which consists of four functional blocks, i.e. I/O request subroutines, I/O initialisation control, interrupt control and timing control. The solid lines show the control flow and the dotted lines show the information flow among the various blocks.

Each of these block functions as follows:

(a) A user program first stores some information in the I/O transaction memory block (IOTR), such as the I/O unit number, the data length to read/write, the data address in the main memory etc. It then issues an I/O command, using one of the I/O request macros.

(b) The I/O request macro calls the corresponding I/O request subroutine. The subroutine accepts the request, edits necessary I/O commands called channel command words (CCWs) and stores them in a specific area in the main memory. It then attaches the IOTR to the I/O execution queue. Then, the control is temporarily transferred to the top of the base level control program (TOP1). Incidentally, Table 3.1 shows an example of the typical I/O request subroutines for the DRIOCS.

(c) The I/O initialisation control program, activated at proper intervals (typically 12 ms for DRIOCS), checks the I/O state and sends a command (SIO command) to initialise the data channel equipment. The data channel equipment, once initiated by the SIO command, commences to operate as a data transmission control processor in place of the central control. It reads the CCWs stored in the specific words of the main memory one after another and sends/receives the designated length of data to/from the designated I/O unit from/to the designated area in the main memory. When it completes all designated commands in the CCWs, it fires an interrupt source flip-flop to inform the central control of the completion of the I/O requests.

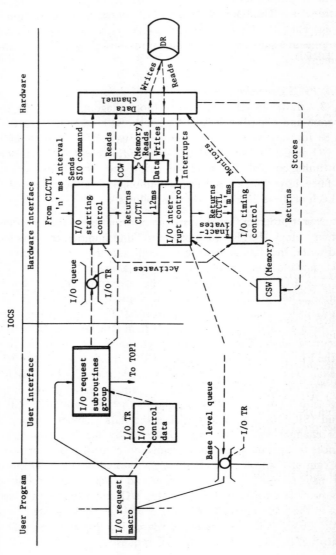

Fig. 3.7   IOCS functional block diagram

(d) The interrupt control program, activated at 12 ms intervals, looks at the I/O interrupt source flip-flops. When it finds the 'fired' flip-flop it identifies the corresponding IOTR with the various information previously stored in the specific words (CSWs) by the data channel equipment. The IOTR is then attached to a queue to inform the user program of the completion of the I/O request.

Table 3.1   *Example of DRIOCS I/O request subroutines*

Subroutine	Function
DRRD	Reads a designated length of data from a designated area in the DR memory (ACTDR) and stores them in a designated area in the main memory
DRWT	Reads a designated length of data from a designated area in the main memory and stores them in a designated area in both the ACTDR memory and the SBYDR memory
DRCPY	Reads a designated length of data from a designated area in the ACT (SBY) DR memory and stores them in a designated area in the SBY (ACT) DR memory

Note: ACT Active
SBY Standby

(e) The timing control program counts clocks to monitor the reasonable operation time of both the data channel equipment and the I/O unit. The count is activated by the I/O initialisation control program when it starts the data channel equipment and inactivated by the interrupt control program when it identifies the I/O request completion. If the count exceeds some value, the timing control program regards the relevant hardware as being in some trouble and calls a fault processing program for a further fault analysis.

(f) Afterwards, the base level control program detaches the IOTR from the queue and returns the control to the next address where the user program issued the I/O request command.

3.7 Clock management

In a switching system, a 'clock' is used for many purposes. For example, it is used for a charge recording feature to record a call origination time, an answer time, a disconnection time, a call duration time etc., for printing a date in typed messages and for a program activation control for some programs which are scheduled to be activated at a specific hour in a day, or a specific day in a month etc.

The clock is generated by the software, based on the 4 ms clock interrupt. The clock management program counts the 4 ms clock interrupts and stores the result in specific words in the memory to form a clock called 'software clock'. In addition, the system provides another clock facility called 'hardware clock' to support the software clock.

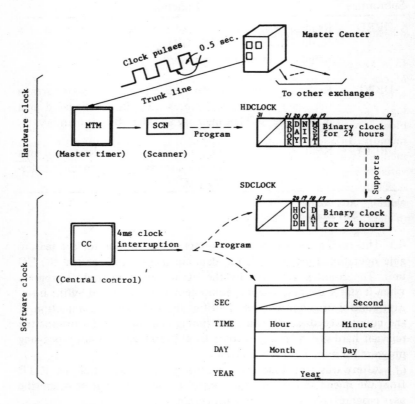

Fig. 3.8   *Clock facility*

Fig. 3.8 shows a configuration of both the software clock and the hardware clock. The master timer circuit (MTM) counts clock pulses of 0·5s duration and 1 second cycle, which are supplied from a master centre through a trunk line, and presents the result at a scanner input. A program reads the trunk scanner and stores the result in the HD-CLOCK word to form a 24 hour binary clock of 0·5s multiples. The software clock consists of 2 different types. One is the SDCLOCK which is very similar to the HDCLOCK and is generally used for a charge recording feature. The other is an 'absolute clock' to show the present absolute time in a year. As shown in the Figure, the absolute time is shown in four words, i.e. the SEC word to show 'second', the TIME word to show 'hour' and 'minute', the DAY word to show 'month' and 'day' and the YEAR word to show 'year'. The absolute time clock is mainly used for printing a date in typed messages.

3.8 Memory management

In a switching program, memory blocks called *transaction memory blocks* are used by many programs. For instance, these blocks are used when a program transfers data to another program for further processing. The D-10 program provides several kinds of transaction memory block. These blocks are collectively pooled in a specific area in the main memory. In addition some memory space is also reserved in the drum memory for shared use in applications such as subscriber class words, variable abbreviated dialing list, multihunting list etc. (see Chapter 10).

These memory blocks both in the main memory and in the drum memory are managed by a special group of programs called 'memory management programs' for efficiently using the memory space.

3.9 Transaction memory block management

Table 3.2 lists all transaction memory blocks used in the D-10 program. As shown in the table, each word length of the transaction memory blocks varies from a minimum of 4 words to a maximum of 1024 words. In particular the universal transaction block (UTR) has a total of six types of blocks with different block size. Generally, it is more efficient to have one common memory pool for all these blocks than to have a separate memory pool for each of the blocks. However, it should be noted that total common use of a memory pool may cause some problems. These problems can occur where a transaction block request traffic may be greatly biased to a specific blocks to an extent that the memory pool remains too small for any other blocks. Hence, the D-10 system actually employs a compromise solution in that all transaction blocks are divided into 4 groups each of which has its own memory pool, as shown in the table.

Fig. 3.9 shows an example of actual memory management tables for the universal transaction memory block (UTR). The UTR memory pool

Table 3.2 *Transaction memory blocks*

Transaction block name	Block class (SCL)	Block size (words)	Memory pool size	Objective
HPTR (Hopper transaction memory block)	0	4	4 × 32 (128 words)	To activate various base level task programs
CPTR (Call processing transaction memory block)	1 2	128 256	128 × 6 (2048 words)	To store speech path orders and other miscellaneous informations
TSKTR (Task transaction memory block)	3	128	(Common to CPTR and TSKTR)	To read overlay task tables
GTR (General purpose transaction memory block)	4	32	32 × 2 (64 words)	To output 'self-control' messages
UTR (Universal transaction memory block)	5 6 7 8 9 10	32 64 128 256 512 1024	32 × 64 (2048 words)	To read/write data from/to teletypewriter units, read overlay programs from drum memory and activate diagnostic programs

consists of two groups, MP0 and MP1. Each of the MP0 and the MP1 consists of 1024 consecutive words and are further divided into 32 small blocks of 32 words. Thus, a total of 64 small blocks of 32 words are contained in the UTR memory pool Each bit in IDLFT table is an *idle flag* to indicate the state of the corresponding transaction block. Two words of the IDLFT table are assigned for the UTR memory pool. Each bit of the first word (2nd word) shows the state of the corresponding small block in the MP0 (MP1). The MPA table contains address data to point the corresponding memory pool head address.

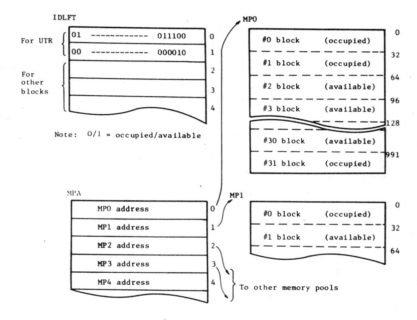

Fig. 3.9 *Example of memory management data for universal transaction blocks (UTR)*

The memory management program actually works as follows:

(*a*) A user program requests the memory management program to obtain a transaction block, using a macro instruction as follows:

$$GTM \ X \ \triangle\triangle\triangle$$

where X shows a memory pool name, and $\triangle\triangle\triangle$ shows a block size.

Assume that a user program requires a 64-word UTR it issues a macro instruction as GTMU064.

(*b*) The memory management program fetches the corresponding two words from the IDLFT table. It searches for a pair of bits that are consecutively 0 in the two words to find two consecutively available small blocks.

(*c*) When it finds a pair of '0' bits, it modifies either MP0 head address or MP1 head address with the number of the found bits position, and thus determined the address of a 64-word UTR.

(*d*) It changes the two bits into 11 (binary) in the IDLFLT table to make the UTR an occupied state.

(*e*) Next, it stores the block class (SCL see Table 3.2) in the UTR. This data is used later when the UTR is freed.

(*f*) Then, it returns the control to the user program with the address data of the UTR in a specific register.

Thus, a user program can easily obtain a transaction block by simply using a macro instruction. The user program can also easily return a transaction block to the memory pool by similarly using a FTM macro. The memory management program works in a reverse way to the above.

Memory management is the drum memory
In the drum memory, a total of 3 kinds of memory pools are provided. They are 5 words multiple pool, 10 words multiple pool and 100 words multiple pool and are used for auxiliary blocks of subscriber class words, variable abbreviated dialling lists and multihunting lists respectively (Chapter 10). All of these pools are also managed by the memory management programs in almost the same manner as the above case.

Chapter 4

Call processing programs

4.1 Introduction to call processing

Call processing consists of two categories of tasks. One is *supervision* which consists of monitoring the line and various trunk circuits looking for signals which indicate requests for some form of action (such as set-up a call, number dialled, recall an operator and so on). The point of supervision changes with the phase of a connection. In the idle state, the supervision point is the subscriber's line circuit and in other states, the point of supervision is one of the various trunk circuits.

The other class of task is *execution* which takes the detected signals, deduces the required operation to execute the request and issues the necessary commands to satisfy the request. Fig. 4.1 shows examples of these two types of tasks applied to a simple intraoffice call.

While a subscriber is in the idle state, the supervision point is the line circuit and the system monitors this point looking for a change in the line current from OFF to ON. This indicates a call origination request. When the system detects this request, it executes a task to set up a path between the calling subscriber and an originating register trunk (ORT). The supervision point is then transferred to the OGT so the line current state is monitored via a trunk scanner.

The ORT supervision task looks for dial pulses and converts them into decimal digits. Once it is detected that dialling is complete, the system executes a task to set up the type of connection implied by the dialled code. In our example, this is a simple intraoffice call. In this case a task is executed which performs four main functions:

(i) the path to the ORT is cleared

(ii) a path is found and reserved between calling and called subscribers via an intraoffice trunk (IOT)

(iii) a ringing current generator trunk (RGT) is connected to the called subscriber

(iv) a ring back tone trunk (RBT) is connected to the calling subscriber

The supervision points of the calling and called subscriber are moved to the RBT and RGT circuits and the system monitors for either an

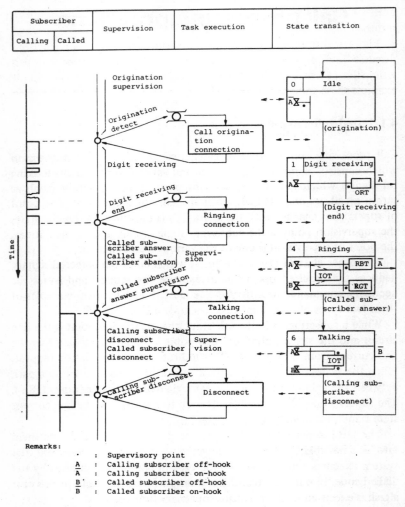

Remarks:

·	:	Supervisory point
$\underline{A}$	:	Calling subscriber off-hook
$\overline{A}$	:	Calling subscriber on-hook
$\underline{B}$	:	Called subscriber off-hook
$\overline{B}$	:	Called subscriber on-hook

Fig. 4.1 *Call progress and switching operation*

answer condition by the called subscriber or a clear from the calling subscriber.

When an answer signal is detected, the talking connection task is executed which establishes the previously reserved path between calling and called subscribers and clears the connections from RGT and RBT.

The supervision points of the calling and called subscribers are moved to either side of the IOT. When a disconnect signal from calling subscriber is detected, the disconnect task is executed which returns both subscribers to idle and releases the path and IOT. Supervision is returned to the subscriber line circuits.

Fig. 4.1 also shows a very powerful method of describing the actions discussed above. The different periods for which the system is supervising the call may be identified as 'states' of the call. In our simple example these states are:

> Idle
> Digit reception
> Ringing
> Talking

Within each state it is very useful to provide a diagrammatic representation of the equipment involved in the call. The basis for this is shown in Fig. 4.2. The line and trunk link networks are represented by single lines and any paths and trunks involved are also shown. A dotted line indicates that a path has been reserved but is not made. The points of supervision are noted by a dot. A call is only going to change state when some signal is received and these signals can be represented by labelled lines emanating from a state box.

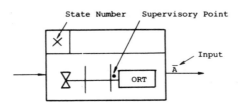

Fig. 4.2 *State-transition diagram expression*

In general, in any one call state there can be more than one relevant signal. For instance, in the digit reception or ringing state, the signal of calling party disconnect may be received. These additional signals require the state of the call to move to *idle* rather than the next state.

This now gives us what is called a *state-transition diagram* which describes a sequential automaton. This is a machine whose output is dependent not only upon its input but on some function of the history

Table 4.1 *State-transition concept definitions*

Call state and state number (State)	The stable state in the call procedure; that is, the state while a switching exchange is supervising and waiting for the next request signal is defined as a 'call state'. A 'state number' is given to each individual call state.
Task and task number (Output)	The switching operation procedure required for transition from one call state to another is defined as a 'task'. A 'task number' is given to each individual task.
Task initiating event (Input)	The process request which causes a state transition is called a 'task initiating event', which consists of an input signal and its supervisory point such as a calling and/or a called subscriber.

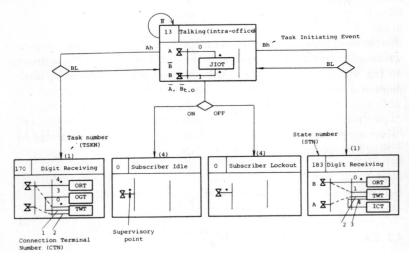

Speech path expression

Solid line: Connected path
Dotted line: Reserved path in memory (Not connected but made-busy for next connection)

Symbol
A   : Off-hook state of a calling subscriber
B   : Off-hook state of a called subscriber
$\bar{A}$: On-hook state of a calling subscriber
$\bar{B}$: On-hook state of a called subscriber
Ah   : Calling subscriber hooking
Bh   : Called subscriber hooking
$\bar{B}_{t.o}$: Disconnecting timeover of a called subscriber on-hook
◇   : Branch symbol
BL   : Blocked state due to trunk or link busy

Fig. 4.3 *Example of state-transition diagram*

of previous inputs. The relevant history of previous inputs is expressed by the state.

The state-transition diagram as applied to the telephone call provides a direct definition of the tasks to be executed on receipt of any particular signal since the task must modify the connection pattern between the originating and terminating states. This is summarised in Table 4.1.

A typical example of a state-transition diagram is shown in Fig. 4.3. This diagram is related to the transitions from the talking state (state number is 13) in an intraoffice connection. There are two supervisory points, a calling side and a called side in the JIOT; therefore, there are four task initiating events in the talking state either on-hook or hook flash from each side. In the talking state, when a called subscriber's on-hook is detected prior to that of a calling subscriber's, the disconnect operation is executed after the preset timing count. This timing state is combined with the talking state by using software design techniques for reduction of the number of call states. The D-10 system is described with approximately 700 states and 2000 tasks, some parts of which are shown in the Appendix.

The advantages of introducing the state-transition concept are summarised as follows:

(i) The functional specification of a switching exchange can be expressed easily and accurately by means of state-transition diagram. In other words, it is useful as a specification description language.

(ii) In addition to the specification description, the state transition diagram can provide a powerful design method for call processing; that is, it is located near the top of '*top-down*' software design methods.

4.2 Call processing program control flow

There is a direct mapping from the state-transition diagram specification of call processing into a software structure. This is shown in Fig. 4.4 and consists of three elements:

(*a*) *Input programs:* These are a group of cyclic programs which periodically monitor active supervision points looking for input signals. There are about 25 programs provided, the number depends upon the types of input signals used. Each input program is activated at its own rate, examines the changes in various signalling conditions and detects input signals. When an input signal is detected, the input program records the signal plus the identity of the item of equipment on which it occurred in a hopper transition memory (HPTR). The input program requests internal processing for the call by attaching the HPTR to a base level queue.

(*b*) *Internal processing program:* The internal processing program consists of an analysis program and a task execution program.

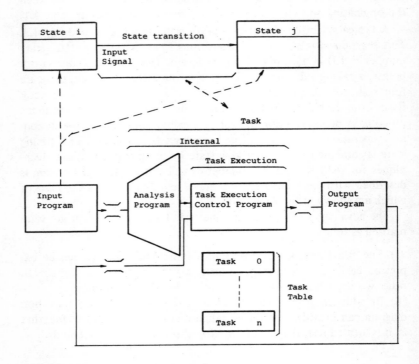

Fig. 4.4.   *Diagram of call-processing flow*

(i) *Analysis program:* The analysis program makes a decision as to the required task based on the input signal and the current call state. When the analysis program requires subscriber class data stored on the drum, it suspends the processing of that call until the data has been obtained from the subscriber data file on the magnetic drum memory.

(ii) *Task execution program:* In the D-10 system, there is a separate task program for each combination of valid input signal and state. There are over 2000 such tasks and it is necessary to use a programming technique to conserve program memory size and to simplify the programming processes. Each task consists of a series of components such as selecting a speech path, operating a relay, updating a traffic counter and so on. The technique used in D-10 is to define a task as a series of task macros, which accomplish the required task. A total of about 150 such macros types are required and typically a single task consists of around ten macros. The use of macros simplifies the programming and program size is reduced by the use of interpretive code (The interpretive code technique use is discussed in detail below). The task execution program is responsible for interpreting the stored macros and executing them.

(*c*) *Output program:* The output program transmits the output orders that are produced by the internal processing program to the corresponding speech path equipment, and tests the results of the operation. After completing the speech path equipment control, the output program returns the control to the internal processing program to make it accomplish the final processing for the call state transition, such as setting supervision conditions in a new state. In addition, the output program includes a digit-sending function and a meter-pulse sending function.

4.3 Call processing data organisation

The data used may be classifed as follows:

Supervision control data for input and output processing: There is a supervision control memory, called '*supervisory memory*' (SM), that is provided for every terminal (trunk or subscriber line). This supervisory memory is used for detecting input signals or identifying output signal sending requests.

Speech path equipment busy-idle state indication data: Busy or idle state indication memory is provided for every link in the switch (called a '*map*') and for every trunk (called a '*trunk idle chain*'), etc. These are used for the speech path selection process.

Call record data: Call record data is required to store the data associated with an individual call. The volume of data needed varies with the call state. Also there is much higher volume of data required whilst a call is in the process of a state transition as compared to a stable state. To achieve efficient use of call record data storage, the data on an individual call is stored in a number of separate memory blocks which are chained together for the time for which they are needed. The types of memory blocks used are as follows:

(*a*) *Trunk memory (TRM)*
A trunk memory is permanently provided for every trunk circuit in the system. The trunk memory block for a general trunk consists of 2 words, 32 bits wide with the basic layout of data as shown in Fig. 4.5.

It contains the basic call data, such as the call state number, the subscriber class data, the identity of a speech path used in connecting a call etc.

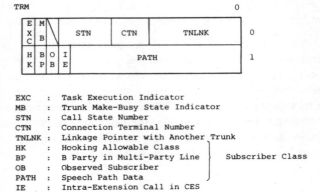

EXC   : Task Execution Indicator
MB   : Trunk Make-Busy State Indicator
STN   : Call State Number
CTN   : Connection Terminal Number
TNLNK : Linkage Pointer with Another Trunk
HK   : Hooking Allowable Class
BP   : B Party in Multi-Party Line   } Subscriber Class
OB   : Observed Subscriber
PATH   : Speech Path Data
IE   : Intra-Extension Call in CES

Fig. 4.5   *Trunk memory*

For special service trunks, such as originating or incoming register trunks, outgoing sender trunks, metering trunks etc. a larger trunk memory block is provided to store such things as dialled number, connection time and so on. When a call is in a stable state, the associated trunk memories contain all the information required for that call. However, when a call requires task execution, further memory blocks have to be used.

(*b*) *Timing register memory (TMR)*
A timing register memory is provided to monitor hit-timing, hooking timing etc. A timing register memory block, which consists of 5 words, is seized and used when the occasion arises.

(*c*) *Transaction memory (TR)*
A transaction memory is used to deliver various call-processing data from one program to another while the task execution is in process. There are several types of transaction memories, as shown in Table 3.2. For example, the hopper transaction memory (HPTR), the call processing transaction memory (CPTR) and the task transaction memory are mainly used in call processing.

According to the call category and the progress of the call process several trunks may be associated with one call. Moreover, the TMR or the TR may also be associated with the call while the task is being executed. On the other hand, the call processing program needs to access all data associated with the call concerned. Therefore, all memory blocks associated with the same call must be linked up with one another.

This linkage of related memory blocks is achieved by using the 'cyclic-chain' method. In this method, all associated trunks are linked cyclically, by recording one trunk's TN (trunk number) in another trunk's TRM, as shown in Fig. 4.6.

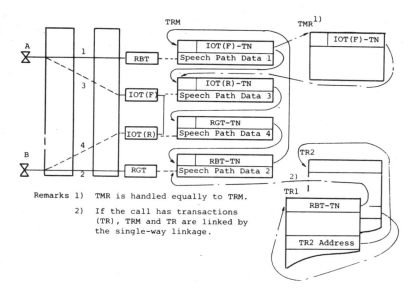

Remarks 1)   TMR is handled equally to TRM.

2)   If the call has transactions (TR), TRM and TR are linked by the single-way linkage.

Fig. 4.6   *Trunk memory cyclic linkage*

When the TMR is associated with a call, it is handled in just the same way as the TRM and then linked into the cyclic-chain. Furthermore, when some transaction memory blocks are united during the process of a task execution, these transaction memory blocks will have a source TN, which starts the task. This is called single-way linkage from the TR to the TRM. However, several transaction memory blocks associated with the same call are linked with one another in the cyclic chain.

(*d*) *Translation data*

Various kinds of translation data are provided such as originating subscriber translation data, terminating subscriber translation data, exchange code translation data, trunk class translation data, various equipment number translation data etc.

4.4 Implementation of call processing

4.4.1 Review of call processing method

We can now summarise the action of call processing. When a call is in a stable state the information relating to it is stored in the trunk memories. The trunk memories related with one call are connected together by a cyclic linkage. During a transition process, beside the trunk memories, a transaction memory (TR) is assigned to this call and a common buffer area, (the 'task execution memory' (TEM)) is used as a scratch pad by the internal program. This process is illustrated in Fig. 4.7.

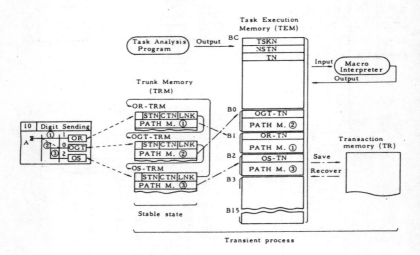

Fig. 4.7   *Call processing memory plan*

When an input program finds an event, an identifier of the call and the event code are registered in a transaction memory through a queue to wait for internal process, and then a task is triggered. The first internal processing program is a task analysis program, which accesses the trunk memories and reads out state number (STN) and connected terminal number (CTN). Then, using this information and the event code as input, the program looks up task decision tables to choose the required task. As a result of the process, the next state number (NSTN), task number (TSKN), and if necessary, outgoing trunk group number (TGN), etc. are stored at specified positions in the TEM.

Program control is then transferred to the task execution program. Before beginning execution of the specified task, it also accesses the cyclic linkage and transfers information, which may be used for task execution, from the trunk memories to memory blocks (Bi) of TEM corresponding to CTN. When this initialisation has completed, a specified task execution is started by interpreting the macros one by one.

When the execution reaches a macro which requires speech path control or I/O control, the macro execution is suspended until these actions complete. During the suspended time, a part of the information in TEM is saved in TR and recovered at a restart point.

When the task execution has finished, the call is completely transferred in to the next stable state, and again put under supervision of input programs.

4.4.2 Task language

In D-10 call processing, a macro language called Task language (TL) is adopted. The TL consists of task decision language (TDL) and task execution language (TEL).

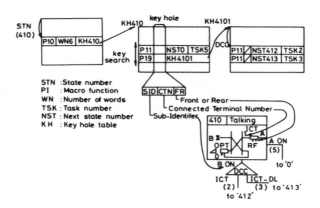

STN : State number
PI : Macro function
WN : Number of words
TSK : Task number
NST : Next state number
K H : Key hole table

Fig. 4.8   *Task decision table format*

TDL is used to write task decision tables and describes the process of deciding a task using a state number, an event code and other attributes of call. An example of this is shown in Fig. 4.8 with the following meanings:

PI0   WN6, KH410

This means to search key hole table KH410, which has 6 words, with input key.

PI1   ON, CTN1, F, NST0, TSK5

If the input key matches the key hole, namely, ON, CTN1, F,

task decision is completed. Task number 5 and next state number 0 are output to TEM.

PI9   ON, CTN0, R, KH4101

If the input key matches the key hole, namely, ON, CTN0, R, look up the next table KH4101 by indexing a disconnecting class (DCC) of the trunk circuit.

The example in Fig. 4.8 shows the following action of the system. The call in STN410 is an incoming call to a CENTREX extension line which was set up with the assistance of an attendant in CENTREX service. When the calling subscriber requests disconnection, which can be detected by a disconnect signal on the ICT front side, the next state number can be uniquely decided as '0'. In the case of a called subscriber hanging up his handset, the next state differs according to whether an incoming trunk has a ringing control function or not. Therefore, further table expansion with the trunk class DCC is necessary.

In general, event codes detected by input programs are used directly as inputs for the decision tables, but dialled digits are condensed by translator before being applied to a task decision (as described in Chapter 6). The number of task decision macros is shown in Table 4.2.

Table 4.2 *Number of task macros*

	Number of task decision macro	Number of task execution macro
Common	5	49
Local stage	90	86
Toll stage	18	24
Total	113	159

TEL is used to write the actual switching functions. As shown in Table 4.2, local switching functions can be represented by 135 TEL macros, whereas toll switching functions can be represented by 73. Table 4.3 shows a partial TEL set with actual parameters.

An example of a task that performs an outgoing connection is shown in Fig. 4.9. According to the sequence number in this Figure, the action of TEL is briefly explained.

(1) Based on the trunk group number stored in TEM, hunt for an idle OGT and then hunt for a network path between the selected OGT terminal and subscriber terminal specified by the content of BO and store this path information into B1. If it happens to encounter a blocking condition of either OGT or network path, then go to JO and request a task which will send a busy tone.

(2) Transfer subscriber's class of service information from the originating register memory to the outgoing trunk memory.

(3) Hunt for an idle outgoing sender (OS), and then hunt for a network path between the OS and OGT terminals. Store this path information into B2.

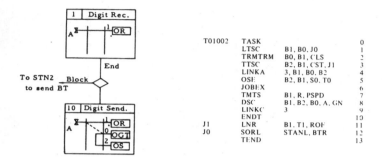

T01002	TASK		0
	LTSC	B1, B0, J0	1
	TRMTRM	B0, B1, CLS	2
	TTSC	B2, B1, CST, J1	3
	LINKA	3, B1, B0, B2	4
	OSE	B2, B1, S0, T0	5
	JOBEX		6
	TMTS	B1, R, PSPD	7
	DSC	B1, B2, B0, A, GN	8
	LINKC	3	9
	ENDT		10
J1	LNR	B1, T1, ROF	11
J0	SORL	STANL, BTR	12
	TEND		13

Fig. 4.9   *Example used for Table 4.3*

(4) Link trunk memories in the order of OGT, OR, OS and again OGT cyclically, and write the new STN and CTN by the reassigned order of the linkage. That is, 0 for OGT, 1 for OR and so on.

(5) Edit the speech path control orders to connect OGT and OS, and write them into TR.

(6) Attach the TR in a queue for execution of the output command.

(7) Stop permanent signal and partial dial timing on OR.

(8) Transfer the dialled digits from OR to OS and request outpulsing program to send digits to the next office.

(9) Make an access to the cyclic linkage and clear an indicator (gate bit) in each trunk memory that was set to inhibit reception of any new event during the task execution. The transition between states is now completed and the call is under the supervision of an input program.

4.4.3 Use of interpretive code

The number of different macros required is shown in Table 4.2. They total less than 256 and generally their parameters are obtained from specific locations in the task execution memory (either directly or indirectly). It is, therefore, possible to completely specify a macro instruction within one computer word by allocating 8 bits to specify the required macro, 4 bits to specify a register (B0 to B15) and so on. This word may be interpreted to produce the required actions.

Since a task contains an average 17 macros, only 17 words are

Table 4.3 *A partial task execution language set*

Function	An example of parameters	Brief function explanation
LTSC	B1, B0, BTT, J3	Hunt a trk. in specified group, then, hunt a path from it to specified line
TTSC	B0, B2, RBT, J5	Hunt a trk. in specified group, then, hunt a path from it to specified trk.
LLC	B3, B2, J1, J2	Hunt a path between specified lines
LNR	B2, T1, FON, N	Make idle specified trk. and path, and set supervisory function for this trk.
LLR	B1, B2	Make idle specified path between lines
VLLC	B2, B1, J5	Hunt a video path between specified lines
VLLR	B1, B2	Make idle specified video path between lines
TKSEL	B2, B3, RBT, J2	Hunt a trk. in specified group
TKIDL	B0, FOF	Make idle specified trk. and set supervisory function for it
ALNKC	B8	Make idle or make busy specified A-link of network
SMCU	B2, RON	Set supervisory function for specified trk.
RTS	B0	Initialise specified originating or incoming register
DSC	B1, B3, B2, A, TSGN	Transfer dialled digit from specified OR to OS for outpulsing
CHPSC	B0	Activate a meter pulse sending function of specified trk.
STNS	B2, STN92	Set specified STN to specified trk. memory
LINKA	3, B0, B2, B1	Link specified trks in specified order, and set STN and CTN into them
TMTS	B1, S, PSPD	Set specified timing to specified trk.
TRMTEM	B5, TRM, TNLINK, BC, TN	Transfer specified data in specified trk. memory to TEM
TRMTRM	BC, MB1, B3, TOGM, MB1	Transfer specified data in TEM to specified Bi
LLO	B2	Idle specified line
MCLA	B0	Store clock information into specified trk. memory as an answering time for charging

Table 4.3 *contd.,*

Function	An example of parameters	Brief function explanation
MCLB	B1, B0	Account charge information for specified trk. and add it to specified charge meter
JOBEX	J9	Execute speech path and I/O control
SORL	STANLP, BTR	Return to specified task analysis program
CJMP	J2, C1	Conditional jump to specified point
TNOP		No operation (for debugging)
ENDT		End of the task (transfer control to ECP)
ICTE	B1, B2, S5, T4	Edit specified control orders for specified incoming trk.
OGTE	B2, B5, S10, T5	Edit specified control orders for specified out-going trk.
OSE	B2, B1, S2, TO	Edit specified control orders for specified out-going sender
IOTE	B5, B2, S5, T2	Edit specified control orders for specified intraoffice trk.
BTE	B0, B2, S5, T8	Edit specified control orders for specified busy tone ckt.

required to store it. Typically such a task written in executable assembly code occupies 220 words.

Therefore, by a simple comparison, interpretative execution decreases the necessary memory capacity by up to one thirteenth.

4.4.4 Run-time comparison of assembly code and interpretive code

Writing tasks in assembly language, the average number of instruction cycles to process each task can be decreased from 1110 with interpretive code to 625. Therefore, interpretive code requires about 78% extra execution time to process a task, compared with assembly language. This corresponds to a 22% rise in system overall run-time, as shown in Fig. 4.10.

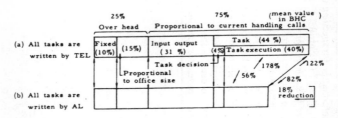

Fig. 4.10   *Analysis of CPU processing time*

This time utilisation inefficiency can be analysed as follows:

(*a*) Extra steps needed for generality and standardised interface occupy about 50% of the total inefficiency.

(*b*) Standardised initialisation of the trunk execution memory requires extra steps, which occupy about 26% of total inefficiency.

(*c*) Inefficiency raised from interpreting the macro orders and their parameters occupies about 24%.

As a result, it may be seen that the use of interpretive code reduces call-handling capacity by less than 22% (excluding the speed up option discussed below), and saves memory in the range of from one half to one thirteenth.

4.4.5 Traffic-handling-capacity improvement

Although a wide variety of services is offered by an SPC exchange system, most of its traffic load is concentrated on some simple services. Fig. 4.11 shows the cumulative traffic distribution against tasks arranged in descending order of traffic in a standard local exchange office. It shows that, out of 2200 tasks in total, the highest 20 tasks carry more than 80% of the total traffic. Based on this characteristic, a small amount of additional memory capacity, which contains the assembly-coded programs for high-traffic tasks, will reduce the traffic-handling-capacity loss caused by use of interpretive code. Fortunately, high-traffic-task categories break down into such simple calls as an outgoing call, an incoming call and an intraoffice call. They are functionally

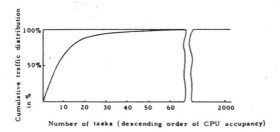

Fig. 4.11   *Cumulative traffic distribution against tasks*

stable, that is, not many changes to them are expected, even if new services are added. Thus, the application of assembly code to these calls will not obstruct the purposes of interpretive code. For these reasons, options are added to the D-10 system to increase the traffic handling capacity, in which 15 tasks are written in assembly code for local switching and 12 tasks for toll switching. In the D-10 local switching, these options reduced its traffic capacity loss to about 4% at the cost of an additional 3·5K words memory. In the D-10 toll switching system, the loss was reduced by adding 2K words memory. These options are realised by a simple procedure, namely by including them in the file and by changing flag bits in corresponding task address tables.

Chapter 5

Input programs

5.1 Subscriber signalling

A subscriber can request a switching operation by means of the hook switch and by dialling. The switching system receives these requests as connect/disconnect state of a DC loop or else an AC signal through a subscriber line. The switching system is provided with scanner equipment and input programs, to supervise the DC/AC signal from a subscriber line or a trunk.

In addition to the supervision of a DC/AC signal, the input programs can count and accumulate the dialled digits and execute pretranslation and timing control.

Input programs can be divided into the following five functional blocks, according to line class and signalling system:

 (i) subscriber line
 (ii) trunks
 (iii) registers
 (iv) operator positions
 (v) common channel signalling system

Subscriber line supervision
The main function for this block is to detect call-origination requests. It also performs the functions of cancellation of the high and dry (H and D) and lock-out situations. H and D occurs when the system is overloaded and wishes to ignore calling signals, lock-out occurs when a subscriber is timed out for not completing a required operation within a specified time.

The line supervisory scan program is activated periodically and scans each line circuit. The form of the line circuit is shown in Fig. 5.1.

The loop current caused by the subscriber's off-hook operates a line relay (LR) in the line circuit. The LR contact (1r) is connected to a scanner matrix of the LSCN which is then driven periodically. In this system, the scan read is '0' at off-hook and '1' at 'on-hook'.

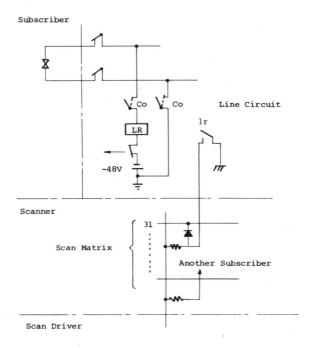

Fig. 5.1 *Line circuit*

Within the central control there is a supervisory memory of one bit for each subscriber allocated to register the 'busy' or 'idle' state of a subscriber. It is called *a line memory (LM)*. It indicates the 'idle' state with LM = '1' and 'busy' state with LM = '0'. A call origination of a subscriber is detected when the value of LM is 'idle' (1) and when the scan result of LSCN is 'off-hook' (0) as shown in Fig. 5.2.

The location at which a subscriber line is connected is called a *line equipment number* (LEN). LEN is expressed by 19 bits, consisting of a network, switch group, grid, switch and level, as shown below.

$$\text{LEN} = X_{18}\,X_{17}\,X_{16}\,X_{15}\,X_{14}\,X_{13}\,X_{12}\,X_{11}\,X_{10}\,X_9\,X_8\,X_7\,X_6\,X_5\,X_4\,X_3\,X_2\,X_1\,X_0$$

| | NW | SG | G | SW | LV |

NW	Network Number	SG	Switch group number
G	Grid number	SW	Switch number
LV	Level number		

This is related to the physical arrangement as shown in Fig. 5.3. In hardware terms, there is one scanner matrix for each 4096 inlets. A

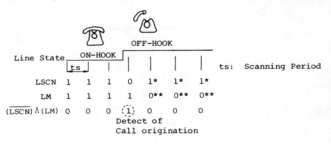

Fig. 5.2   *Call origination detection principle*

  * LSCN becomes '1' because C_0 relay is made open at the time of ORT connection

  ** LM is set to '0' by line supervisory scan program when call origination is detected

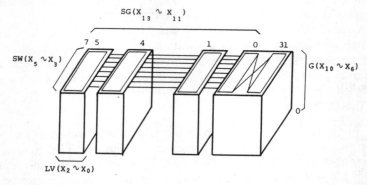

Fig. 5.3   *Line equipment number*

matrix accesses a row of 32 inlets in one instruction (i.e. the size of one computer word) and a complete matrix consists of 128 rows of 32 inlets each. A grid consists of eight 8 × 8 inlets switch so two rows of the scanner matrix are associated with each grid. Each scanner, therefore, serves a total of 64 grids. The relationship between the scanner addressing and the LEN is shown in Fig. 5.4.

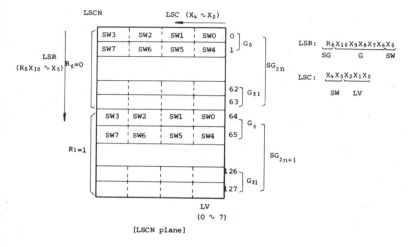

Fig. 5.4 *Correspondence between LEN and LSCN*

The line supervisory scan program function is to detect a call origination and it can be initiated every 200 ms by an execution control program. An outline of this program is shown in Fig. 5.5.

A special instruction is provided in the central control called SUP (search unmatch pattern) to reduce the time overhead associated with this program. This is a 'wired macro' instruction and can execute a series of processes by using only one instruction by using a specially designed logic circuit.

The LSCNP program sets the scanner equipment number, the starting scan row number and the number of scanning rows into the registers in advance. Next, it executes the SUP instruction, by which the specified scanner equipment is driven, and 'logical AND' between the scan result and the line memory is then calculated. When the result of the 'logical AND' contains value '1' bits the SUP instruction will then initiate the FRM instruction in order to decide a bit number value of '1'. This usually corresponds to the originating subscriber. Finally, the LSCNP program can obtain the LEN of an originating subscriber from the scanner equipment number, row number, and the FRM result by referring to the LEN translation table as shown in Fig. 5.6.

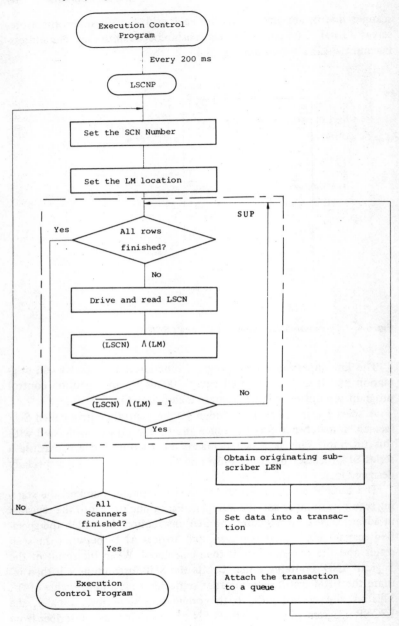

Fig. 5.5   *General flow chart of LSCNP program*

5.2 Dial pulse reception

The functions of the dial pulse reception are divided into the following three categories:

(*a*) detection and counting of a dialled pulse

(*b*) recognition of the interdigit pause and translation of the dialled pulses counted as one digit

(*c*) detection of an abandoned call in the dial reception state.

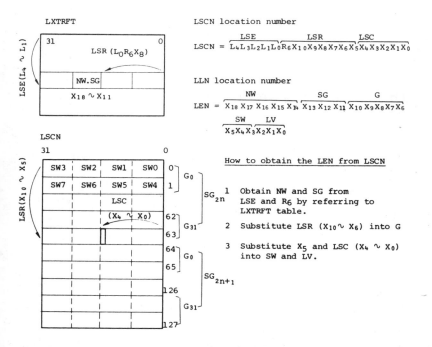

Fig. 5.6   *How to obtain LEN from LSCN*

These functions are realised by scanning a scan point of an ORT in a similar manner to the scanning for an originating call. As illustrated in Fig. 5.7, the minimum width of a dialled pulse is approximately 13 ms, which occurs for a dial speed of 20 ± 2 PPS (pulses per second) and a make ratio of 30%. Therefore, the pulse detection function requires a scan period of less than 13 ms. On the other hand, the other two functions are adequately realised by scanning at a longer interval of about 100 ms. To obtain a high-processing efficiency therefore, these functions are realised by the two programs shown in Fig. 5.8. A dial pulse count program which runs every 8 ms and the DPOR digit store program which runs every 96 ms.

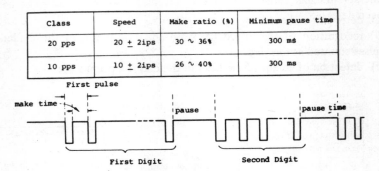

Fig. 5.7   Rotary dialling receiving specification

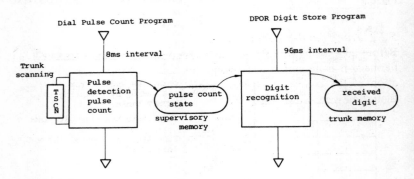

Fig. 5.8   Dial digit receiving

5.2.1 Pulse detection logic

The principle of the pulse detection logic is illustrated in Fig. 5.9. For the detection of a pulse, ORTs are scanned, 32 at a time, by using a SUP (search unmatch pattern) instruction at regular 8 ms intervals. This scan information (SCN) and prescan information (LL: last look) can detect a change in a line state by the following logic equation:

$$(SCN) \oplus (LL) = 1$$

Since this logic equation detects a bidirectional change that is upward and down, the following logic is added so as to detect a change in the downward direction only.

$$(\text{SCN} \oplus \text{LL}) \wedge (\text{ACT}) \wedge (\overline{\text{LL}}) = 1$$

This logic also introduces an ACT bit which means that the logic is only effective when the trunk is in a digit reception state. As a result, when a line state change satisfies the above formula, it means that a pulse has been detected.

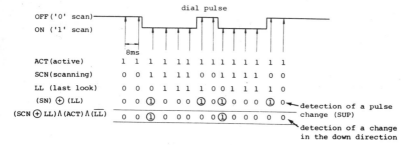

Fig. 5.9 *Pulse detection logic*

5.2.2 *Trunk number configuration*

Before an explanation of the trunk supervisor and scan processing can be made it is necessary to give an explanation of the number configuration of the trunks. A typical example of a trunk number (TN) configuration is shown in Fig. 5.10.

$$\underline{T_{14}\,T_{13}\,T_{12}\,T_{11}\,T_{10}\,T_9\,T_8\,T_7\,T_6\,T_5\,T_4\,T_3\,T_2\,T_1\,T_0}$$

TB: Trunk Block Number
TSG: Trunk Sub-group Number
TU: Trunk Unit Number
TN: Trunk Number

Fig. 5.10 *Trunk number configuration*

First, TB means a block of up to 512 trunks whose supervised logic is the same. That is, the same supervisor program can scan these trunks. A TB consists of up to 16 subgroups called TSG. Each TSG has 32 trunks that can be accommodated in the same row of a scan device. Finally, the TU is the number corresponding to the bit position in a scan device row. Therefore, the TU is determined physically by a particular point in the trunk frame, but TB and TSG can be assigned by appropriate wiring to create easy processing.

5.2.3 Dial pulse count program (DPCNT)

This program requires a very short processing time as it must run frequently at short intervals. Therefore, it uses a highly efficient processing method which can take care of not only the pulse detection of 32 ORTs but also the counting of the detected pulses.

The composition of the pulse counter memory for this processing is shown in Fig. 5.11. There is a 4-bit counter associated with each ORT. Each bit of the counter is allocated at the same bit position in each row. These rows are further separated into 16 words (rows) each. These bits have weights 2^0, 2^1, 2^2 and 2^3 from PC0 to PC3.

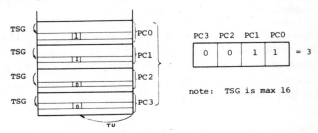

Fig. 5.11 *Pulse counter (PC) in supervisory memory*

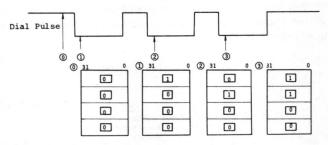

Fig. 5.12 *Pulse count state*

The pulse counting logic that uses this pulse counter is illustrated in Fig. 5.12. The dial pulses are detected at positions ①, ② and ③ in Fig. 5.12, and are added into the counter where the dial number becomes 3.

The logic for processing 32 lines at once used four temporary variable words Ci (i = 0 to 3) which are used for carry information for the 32 lines. Thus the following logic operations are performed on the 32 bit words:

$$PCi = Ci \oplus PCi$$

$$C(i + 1) = Ci \wedge PCi$$

the initial value of C_0 is

$$C_0 = (SCN \oplus LL) \wedge (ACT) \wedge (\overline{LL})$$

and of course

$$PCi = 0$$

Abandon and pause (AP) detection is performed by an AP bit. This bit is set every time a dial break is detected and is used by the digit store program (DPOR) which is described in the next Section. The logic to set the AP bits is

$$AP = (SCN \oplus LL) \wedge (AP)$$

In other words, the AP bit will always set at '1' during the pulse reception. The various words such as LL, ACT, AP and PCi used for the above processing are grouped together into a DPOR supervisory memory as shown in Fig. 5.13. The arrangement has been chosen to ease the processing of 32 line groups.

SM(Supervisory Memory)

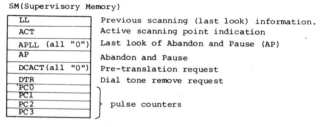

LL	Previous scanning (last look) information.
ACT	Active scanning point indication
APLL (all "0")	Last look of Abandon and Pause (AP)
AP	Abandon and Pause
DCACT(all "0")	Pre-translation request
DTR	Dial tone remove request
PC0	
PC1	
PC2	pulse counters
PC3	

Fig. 5.13 *DPOR supervisory memory structure (each line represents up to 16 words servicing up to 512 lines)*

The dial pulse counter program also deals with the 'dial tone remove request'. At the moment of detection of the first pulse in the first digit from a subscriber the dial tone must be removed. The detection is made by using a 'DTR' bit in SM, according to the following logic equation.

$$DTR = (SCN \oplus LL) \wedge (ACT) \wedge (\overline{LL}) \wedge (DTR)$$

As the DTR bit is set at '1' in the originating call task, the above equation is effective only when the first pulse detection is achieved. After detection of this pulse, this program sets the DTR at '0' and loads the necessary information in the hopper transaction block which then requests the relay operation to remove the dial tone, via the state analysis program.

5.2.4 DPOR digit store program (ORDGST)

The main function of this program is to store the digit, counted in the pulse counter of the SM into the ORT-trunk memory. To realise the above function, it is necessary to recognise the interdigit pause. This is done with the aid of the AP (abandon and pause) bit. This bit is set whenever a line state change is detected. The ORDGST program examines this bit every 96 ms and if it remains zero for two successive 96 ms scans then there can have been no change on the line for between 96 ms to 192 ms. The ORDGST program maintains an APLL (AP last look) word for each 32 lines and every 96 ms checks for

$$\overline{AP} \wedge APLL = 1$$

and then performs $APLL = AP$

$$AP = 0$$

The ORDGST then performs a digit store (and reset of digit counter) for any line for which there had been no change in the last two 96 ms scans and the current state is make. A typical example of this sequence is shown in Fig. 5.14.

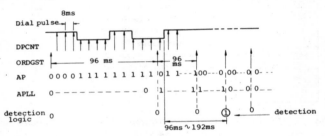

Fig. 5.14   *AP logic state*

If the current state of a no-change line is on-hook the lack of change indicates call abandonment or flashing. Flashing, which consists of a subscriber flashing the hook switch, is permitted in some states and requires additional timing.

An example of a trunk memory with an originating register (ORT) is shown in Fig. 5.15.

When the number of digits received called RDC exceeds the value of a digit count limit (DCL), generally 2, in the trunk memory, a pre-translation program is activated for determining a 'necessary number of digits for digit analysis' (called NND in trunk memory). This program continues the digit receiving until the digit receiving number (RDC) exceeds the value of the NND.

As 'interdigit timing' (4 ~ 5 s) is set up between digits, if the timer indicates time over situation, the received digit counter (RDC) will be compared with the NND. In this case, if the RDC is less than the NND, it means a partial dial and a busy tone connection task is activated. Otherwise, the digit analysis program is activated.

Sometimes there are exchanges in same area where exchange code lengths might be different. What might happen is that there will be a lack of received digits for the digit analysis mainly because the NND is set for smaller figures. In that case, digit reception will continue.

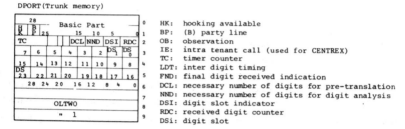

DPORT (Trunk memory)

HK:	hooking available
BP:	(B) party line
OB:	observation
IE:	intra tenant call (used for CENTREX)
TC:	timer counter
LDT:	inter digit timing
FND:	final digit received indication
DCL:	necessary number of digits for pre-translation
NND:	necessary number of digits for digit analysis
DSI:	digit slot indicator
RDC:	received digit counter
DSi:	digit slot

Fig. 5.15 *DP originating register trunk memory*

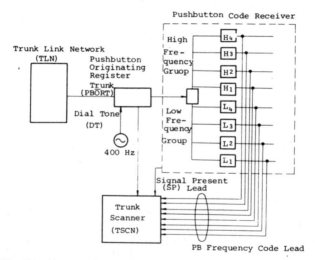

Fig. 5.16 *Hardware configuration for receiving pushbutton codes*

5.3 Pushbutton code reception

Dialling digits from pushbutton telephones are received by a pushbutton receiver (PBREC) and recognised by scanning the associated trunk scan points, as shown in Fig. 5.16. Then, these digits are stored in an associated register trunk memory that is assigned to each pushbutton originating register trunk (PBORT), with an updated digit count.

At that time, it is determined whether the digit pretranslation is necessary or not, according to the digit count. However, if error codes are received, the pushbutton receiving program requests typing out of the information onto the teletypewriter, and then sends a busy tone to the corresponding subscriber line.

The pushbutton code is a 4 by 3 code of audible frequencies. That is, the code consists of a combination of one out of four low frequencies and one out of three high frequencies. It is received by a PBREC and recognised by scanning the associated trunk scan points.

When considering the differences between the receiving characteristics for the seven frequencies, a *signal present* lead (SP) is provided in wired logic in each PBREC, which guarantees the presence of the pushbutton frequency codes. Therefore, before the reading of a pushbutton frequency code, the scanning of the signal present lead and then detecting its status change is performed to determine the presence of the pushbutton signal.

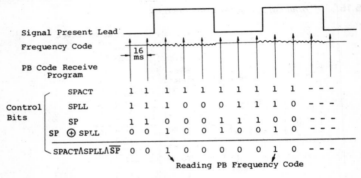

Fig. 5.17   *Decision logic in determining reading timing pushbutton frequency codes*

The pushbutton code receiving program (PBCDRC) is activated every 16 ms and performs the following (Fig. 5.17):

If   SP $\oplus$ SPLL $= 1$ then SPLL $=$ SP

If   SPACT $\wedge$ SPLL $\wedge \overline{\text{SP}} = 1$ then read PB scan points, convert to binary coded decimal and store in PBORT trunk memory

SPLL is the SP last look and SPACT is the bit indicating whether the register is active.

The PBCDRC program requests a digit analysis after it receives sufficient digits in the same way as that of the dial pulse receiving. When it detects error codes in the process of the digit conversion, it calls the state analysis program to initiate the busy-tone-trunk connection. In addition, it requests typing out of the code errors.

5.4 Pretranslation of dialled codes

In digit translation, it is necessary to decide first how many digits must be received and translated, according to the received number construction. Making this decision is generally possible by interpreting the first 1–3 digits. For example, if the first received digit is '1' (for a special number e.g. police), 3 digits must be received and translated. However, if the first 3 digits are '002' (for an international call), 15 digits at the maximum are required. Such interpretation processing is called *pretranslation*, which decides the necessary number of digits for digit translation.

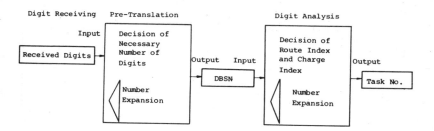

Fig. 5.18   *Received digit translation processing flow*

In addition, pretranslation identifies the calling subscriber's class of service, which is then used to decide the appropriate task in the digit analysis program. It outputs the service identification information that includes what class of subscriber is calling, from what status he is calling, and what service he is requesting. This information is called *digit block string number* (DBSN). A typical example of the processing flow as to the received digit translation is shown in Fig. 5.18.

DBSN is an identifying number assigned to each meaning which is formed by several of the received digits. This idea is analogous with the English language. In other words, in the English language, a word which has some particular meaning is made up of a combination of letters and a sentence is made up of a combination of words. In the same way, the

digit block code (DBC: corresponds to the word) is defined as a combination of received digits, and the DBSN which informs the switching
system of the requested class of service is expressed by a combination
of several DBCs.

However, the DBSN does not include all the DBC combinations.
Each DBC sets a limitation on all other DBCs to some extent. In other
words, there is a kind of grammar utilised just as in the English language.
Some typical examples of DBSNs are shown in Table 5.1.

Table 5.1   *DBSN example*

DBSN	Meaning	Received Digits	QRT/IRT Connection Call Status Number
1	LS, General Dialing	Δ ∿ Δ	3
2	LS, Registration of Abbreviated Dialing	0* □□Δ ∿ Δ	3
3	LS, Video, Registration of Abbreviated Dialing	0* □□* * Δ ∿ Δ	3
4	LS, Abbreviated Dialing	* □□	3
63	Incoming Call by DP Signaling	ΔΔΔΔ	22
64	Incoming Call by MF Signaling	ΔΔΔΔ	26
100	CTX Attendant Dialing (After Holding Outward Line)	(NS) XXXX	374

NS: Number Start button

5.4.1 Determination of the necessary number of digits (NND)

As described previously, the ORDGST program is planned to request
the processing of pretranslation program, invariably after receiving the
first two digits in most general cases. Then, if the received digits are
'10', for example, it is possible to decide the necessary number of
digits directly from those digits, because it is recognised as one of the
subscriber special number calls, like '104'.

On the other hand, in the case of video calls, for example, it is
impossible to decide the number of digits by receiving only two digits
'**'. This is because subsequent digits are required to discriminate a
local call from a long distance call, etc. Therefore, to avoid repeated
and useless pretranslations, the digit count limit (DCL) is generated and
is returned to the ORDGST program (the next request time for pretranslation).

The pretranslation processing is accomplished by the indexing of the digit count length decision tables by the received digits, as shown in Fig. 5.19. This Figure shows the digit count length decision method. When indexing the tables, one after another, by the received digits, the required data will then be found at the location corresponding to the digits. The process indicator (PI) will show the meaning and format of the stored data. For example, 'PI = 2' indicates that you have to index the next table where an address is set in this word by the next digit. This is because the digit count length is not decided yet at this table.

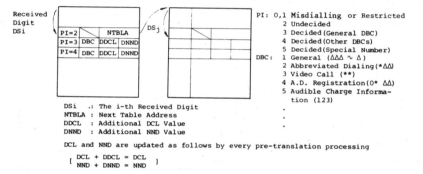

```
DSi   .: The i-th Received Digit
NTBLA : Next Table Address
DDCL  : Additional DCL Value
DNND  : Additional NND Value

DCL and NND are updated as follows by every pre-translation processing

 [  DCL + DDCL = DCL  ]
    NND + DNND = NND
```

Fig. 5.19   *Digit count length decision tables*

However, when 'PI = 3', digit count length is decided and the appropriate processing should now be performed. When this digit count length is decided, the necessary number of digits for digit analysis (NND) and the digit block code (DBC) for the received digits are finally output.

As a result, the obtained NND is set in the trunk memory of the corresponding originating register trunk. Then, digit receiving continues until it receives as many digits as the NND. When the number of received digits is not less than the NND, digit analysis is requested through a pretranslation program.

As shown in Fig. 5.19, the DBC is used to classify the dialling digits functionally, and is used to decide the DBSN according to the class of the originating subscriber. This obtained DBSN is also set in the trunk memory and is used to decide the connection task in the processing of the digit analysis program.

5.4.2 Service identification (DBSN decision)
DBSN is decided from the DBSN decision table, based on the DBC obtained from the digit count length decision table and the class of the

originating subscriber. The DBSN decision tables are divided by the class of the originating subscriber (general, CES* or video), and each subtable is constructed on the basis of the *key search method* with DBC as a key code. The decision method of the DBSN is shown in Fig. 5.20 and an example of DBSN is shown in Table 5.1.

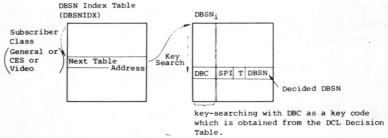

Fig. 5.20   DBSN decision tables

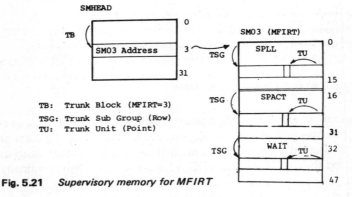

TB: Trunk Block (MFIRT=3)
TSG: Trunk Sub Group (Row)
TU: Trunk Unit (Point)

Fig. 5.21   Supervisory memory for MFIRT

5.5 Trunk signalling input programs

5.5.1 Multifrequency signal reception

Trunk signalling is normally performed by multifrequency tones. A digit is signalled by a combination of two tones selected from 6 tones (this gives a total of 15 values). The multifreqency digits are recognised by scanning a set of scan points which are provided for each multi-frequency incoming register trunk (MFIRT). Then they are converted to digits (binary-coded-decimal representation), and stored as dialled digit information in the trunk memory of the associated MFIRT.

The presence of multifrequency signals is examined by scanning the

* Centralised extension subscriber (i.e. CENTREX)

signal present lead that is provided for by the multifrequency signal receiver and comparing it with the signal present last look bit, in much the same way as in PB code reception. This processing is performed together in a group of 32 MFIRTs. The supervisory memory for the MFIRT consists of SPLL, SPACT and WAIT, as shown in Fig. 5.21.

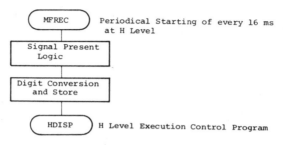

Fig. 5.22 *MF signal receiving program processing flow*

5.5.2 Multifrequency signal reception program (MFREC)
This program consists of signal presence logic processing, digit conversion and digit store processing, as shown in Fig. 5.22.

In the received MF codes, there are KP codes (start of pulsing), dialled digits, ST codes (end of pulsing), and error codes. They are processed as follows:

(*a*) *KP code (start of pulsing):* The KP code is one of the acknowledgment signals used in the seizure sequence and it is necessary to send an ON signal to the calling exchange as an acknowledgment signal for receiving the KP code. Therefore, when a KP code is received, MFREC program hunts a hopper transaction memory (HPTR) and sets the necessary data in it to start the state analysis program which further performs the appropriate processing.

(*b*) *Dialled digits:* When an MFREC program receives dialled digits, it stores them in the trunk memory and updates the received digit count (RDC).

(*c*) *ST code (end of pulsing):* The MFREC program hunts an HPTR, sets the necessary data in it, and then requests a digit analysis. At that time, it sets the end of the digit reception in the corresponding incoming register trunk memory (END = 1). If there are no HPTRs available, it makes this digit analysis request 'wait' by setting the wait bit in the supervisory memory so that it can be processed first at the next processing period. The method of detecting waiting calls is as follows:

$$(\text{SPACT}) \wedge (\text{WAIT}) = 1$$

(*d*) *Error codes:* When error codes are detected, the MFREC program requests the state analysis program to send a busy tone to the corresponding line. It also requests the teletypewriter to type out this information.

Digit conversion can be accomplished by indexing the MF code table directly with the received MF code (coded as a combination of 2 out of 6 frequencies). The MF code table is shown in Table 5.2.

Table 5.2 *Conversion table from received MF code to digit*

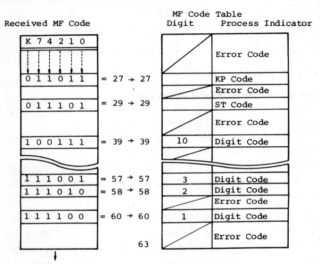

Trunk Scanner Output
(Signal Presence/Absence = 0/1)

5.6 Trunk supervision

There are two main types of signals for telephone call switching; register signals and line signals. Register signal receiving has been described above. Line signal supervision is considered in this Section.

Supervision for changes in call states includes the detection of answer, disconnect, abandonment and some other line signals. Each line signal implies different types of request but they can all be detected by the same method, that is trunk supervision scanning (with the exception of the supervision of incoming trunks by multifrequency signalling for which special traffic control is required). This is performed by the universal trunk supervisory scanning program.

The universal trunk supervisory scanning program (UNSCN) is executed every 96 ms by the L level execution control program. The line condition change detection operates in a similar manner to subscriber line supervisory monitoring. The line condition changes are detected by scanning a trunk scan point (32 at a time) through the trunk scanner and comparing the results with the last-look bit in call store.

The SUP (search unmatch pattern) instruction used for the trunk scanning, differs slightly from that used for the subscriber line scanning because the addresses of the rows of trunk scan points are separated, and so it is necessary to designate a scanning address for each scan.

The processing logic for trunk supervision is as follows:

If $(ACT) \wedge (LL) \wedge (\overline{SCN}) = 1$, then Answer is detected

If $(ACT) \wedge (\overline{LL}) \wedge (SCN) = 1$, then Disconnect is detected

    ACT: Supervisory scanning activation bit
    SCN: Scanning (present state)
     LL: Last look bit (previous state)

This logic is shown in Fig. 5.23.

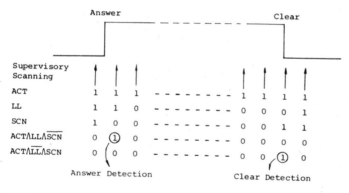

Fig. 5.23 *Answer and clear signals detection logic*

When the universal trunk supervisory scanning program recognises an answer signal, this is reported together with the trunk number, to the state analysis program by attaching a hopper transaction memory to the base level queue. (See Fig. 5.24.)

When the program detects an apparent disconnect signal it is necessary to check that the signal has not been caused by a momentary break on the line. Such momentary breaks are called 'hits' and can occur for many reasons and it is necessary to discriminate these momentary hits from valid changes. This check is achieved by requesting further processing by the hit timing program. This request is produced by attaching a hit-timing register to a hit-timing chain. The hit timing program scans the same trunk scan point in order to confirm that the condition lasts for sufficiently long intervals. (See Fig. 5.24.)

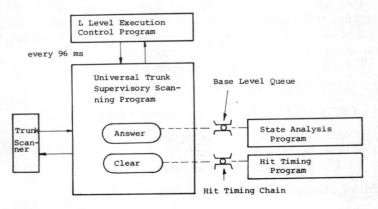

Fig. 5.24   *UNSCN program processing*

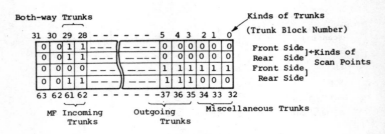

Front Side: Trunk scan point on call originating side in trunks
Rear Side : Trunk scan point on call terminating side in trunks

Fig. 5.25   *Universal trunk supervisory scanning initial data*

In the UNSCN program the scan points that should be scanned are determined by using the universal trunk supervisory scanning initial data. This data defines the trunks of the scanned kind and their trunk scan points, as shown in Fig. 5.25. The scanners themselves are accessed via a look-up table structured as shown in Fig. 5.26.

5.7 Processing of timers

It is necessary to take into consideration the many kinds of timing required for the control of a switching system. The timing classes for call processing are divided by their timing length and precision, as shown in Table 5.3. The different classes require different programs.

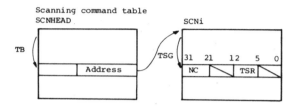

```
TB:    Trunk block number
TSG:   Trunk sub-group number
TSR:   Row number in trunk scanner
NC:    Name code (trunk scanner number)
```

Fig. 5.26 *Scanning command table*

The general method of timing by program utilises a 'timer counter' that is allocated in the trunk memory or somewhere similar and which has indicated a request for a particular type of counting. The timing program decides whether the timing is over or not by decrementing the timer counter at a specific rate and when this counter reaches zero, the timing program executes some predetermined function.

In fact, two different timing methods are used. The choice depends on:

(i) timing length and precision
(ii) type of trunk and the size of its trunk memory
(iii) number of trunks.

One method of timing is the concentration control of a 'request indication of timing processing'. This is called TAC (timer active bit). The other method is called a '*timing chain*'. Two typical examples of a timing program are explained as follows:

(*a*) *Trunk timer program (TRKTIM):* This program is used for timings of approximately 10–20 s. As these timings do not require such high precision, the program can run every 10 s and the timer counter (TC) will be 1 bit and will cover 10–20 s of timing. Some examples of

Table 5.3 *Timings for call processing and examples*

Timing class	Precision	Maximum timing	Timing memory	Feature	Examples
Trunk timer	10 s	10 ~ 20 s	TAC, TC (supervisory memory)	1 Little memory area required for timing (2 bits/trunk)	Forced disconnection timing 10 ~ 20 s
				2 Not so exact	Busy tone sending timing 10 ~ 20 s
				3 Mainly used for numerous trunks, such as speech trunks and miscellaneous trunks	Howler tone sending timing 10 ~ 20 s
Trunk memory	1 s	2 min	TAC (1 bit) TC (7 bits) in TRM	1 It is necessary to add 1 word for timing to TRM	PSPD timing 20 ~ 21 s
				2 More exact (1 s) than 'trunk timer' (10 s)	Digit recognition timing 4 ~ 5 s
				3 Mainly used for register trunks (ORT, IRT)	Delayed call transfer timing 30 ~ 31 s
Timer register timer	2 s	4 min	Timer register (TMR)	1 When timing is necessary, TMR is obtained from common pool and freed after timing is finished	Recorded announcement sending timer 3 min ~ 3 min & half
	10 s	20 min		2 This timer is used for timing that cannot be provided by the trunk timer and/or trunk memory timer	

Table 5.3 contd.,

Timing class	Precision	Maximum timing	Timing memory	Feature	Examples
Hit timing	32 ms	4 s	Timer register (TMR)	When disconnection signal is found, timing by a TMR is necessary to distinguish 'hit from real disconnection	Hit timing 100 ~ 200 ms
Hooking timing	500 ms	64 s	Timer register (TMR)	When hit timing is finished, in case a hooking action is available, more timing by the TMR is necessary to distinguish a hooking from disconnection	Hooking timing 0·1 ~ 1·2 s
Trunk guard timing	1 s	2 s	OGT trunk memory	Obtaining a timing between 1 and 2 s by in-chain and out-chain method	OGT guard timing 0·5 ~ 1 s
SP order execution program	16 ms	512 ms	SP macro order	1 Possible to get a timing within 'ms' level 2 Possible to get a timing during a call state state transition	Timing for inter office signaling Test timing in speech path

this timing are a 'forced disconnection timing' (when a called party hangs up early), and 'tone sending timing'.

A typical example of a memory structure is illustrated in Fig. 5.27. Time-out detection is processed in groups with 32 trunks within one TB and TSG. Its logic equation is:

$$(TAC) \wedge (TC) = 1$$

The program sets TC at 1 for the trunks that are not timed out and will then detect it after 10 s.

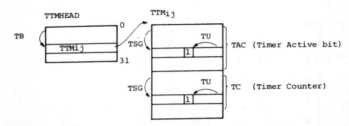

(TAC and TC of each TN are concentrated in a same area)

Fig. 5.27   *'Trunk timer' memory structure*

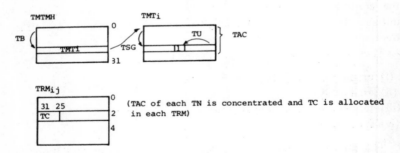

Fig. 5.28   *'Trunk memory timer' memory structure*

(b) *Trunk memory timer program (TRMTIM):* This program provides timing for higher precision and various lengths, such as 'PSPD (permanent signal and partial digit) timing' (10–11 s) and 'delayed call transfer timing' (30–31 s). This program runs every 1 s and times from 1 s to 2 min by counting down a timer counter (TC) having 7 bits in a trunk memory. These 7 bits are part of every trunk memory but they are only used when a request bit is set in an appropriate timing activation control (TAC) memory area (see Fig. 5.28).

Chapter 6

Analysis and translation

6.1 Techniques of analysis

The function of the analysis programs is to analyse the various service requests and decide on the required switching operations or *task*.

The service requests are detected by one of the input or output programs and are recorded into an individual transaction memory block together with the line or trunk number and other call information. These transactions are attached to a base level queue. At the base level the control program detaches the transaction from the queue and initiates the analysis program specified by a starting address stored in the transaction.

There are four classes of analysis program:

  (i) originating subscriber analysis
 (ii) digit analysis
(iii) terminating subscriber analysis
(iv) state analysis

The process of analysis is to perform one or more translations of some appropriate data. For instance, the originating subscriber analysis is a translation from the line equipment number (LEN) to class of service and directory number. The state analysis is a more complex process which translates a combination of signal, current call state, dialled number or other signal, originating subscriber classification etc. into required task and next state. It will be seen later that this type of analysis is achieved by a sequential series of translations.

In a computer there are a number of different methods for translating an input item into one or more output items. The choice of method depends on:

(i) range of possible input values

 (ii) number of valid inputs within range

(iii) variability of size of output items

There are three basic methods:

(*a*) sequential table indexing

(*b*) table look-up

(*c*) associative memory

Economic hardware for the last method does not yet exist so a combination of the first two methods is used. Both these methods regard the information to be translated as a number of items providing a multidimensional index to the required translation. For instance, the dialled digit translation program regards the input information as a series of digit groups.

Sequential table indexing method: In this method, the first item of the input information is used to index a primary table. The primary table has an entry to a secondary table. The secondary table is indexed by the second item and so on. Each entry also contains a process indicator to tell the access program whether the entry corresponds to a pointer to a further table, pointer to a translation or an invalid translation. Fig. 6.1 shows a simple example for a one-stage table.

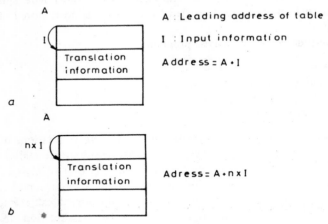

Fig. 6.1 *An example of simplified translation table*
a when one-word information is translated
b when n-word information is translated

Table look-up method: The table look-up method also has multiple tables (in general) but instead of indexing directly to a required entry, each entry itself contains the item of information for which that entry is the full (or partial) translation. This is called a *key hole*. The translation program must therefore access each entry and check whether the item to be translated (i.e. the key) matches the stored item (the key hole). The entry will also contain a progress indicator to allow the translation program to interpret the remaining information in the entry. Fig. 6.2 shows a simple one-stage look-up table. Table look-up is seen to be less efficient in real-time than the indexing method as several memory accesses must be made before a match is found. Naturally, the entries are arranged in decreasing order of probability of access. However, the table look-up method can show considerable memory saving over indexed tables when only a small proportion of the possible values of an item correspond to valid translations. Both methods are used where appropriate in the translation programs of D-10.

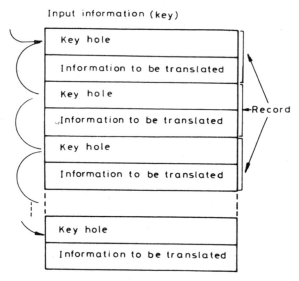

Fig. 6.2   *Table look-up method principle*

6.2 Originating subscriber analysis program (OLANLP)

The originating analysis program generally decides on the type of ORT connection task, including an ORT trunk class and a *route index* (RTX) by analysing the originating subscriber's service class word read from a magnetic drum. In addition, its decision depends on whether the subscriber is hooking or clearing a lock-out.

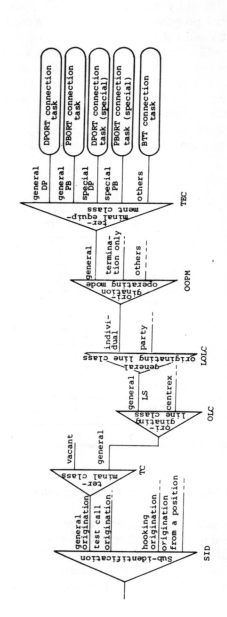

Fig. 6.3   Originating analysis process outline

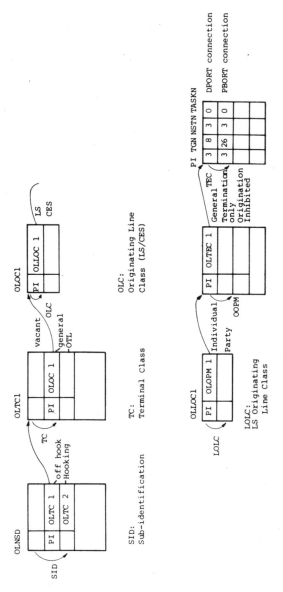

Fig. 6.4 *Originating analysis using a tree structure table origination from subscriber's idle state*

This analysing process to decide upon a task is shown in Fig. 6.3. It is practically implemented by a table logic as shown in Fig. 6.4.

An analysis program searches the table sequentially until the final output information is taken out. A process indicator (PI) in the table shows whether an analysis process is terminated or not. When PI shows analysis termination, a task number is extracted as the final output. In other cases, the next stage of the table is searched according to the address indicated in the table.

Analysing factors, such as subscriber class, are stored at a fixed location within the transaction memory block, as shown in Fig. 6.5. Where necessary the subscriber information is read from a magnetic drum and registered in a transaction memory block.

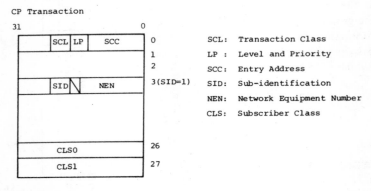

Fig. 6.5 *Input transaction*
General origination

The OLANLP program is initiated by an execution control program in accordance with the indication in the transaction which is detached from a task analysing queue. It continues the analysing process, as described above and finally records the analysis result in a task execution memory (TEM). These results include a next state number (NSTN), a task number (TSKN) and a trunk group number (TGN) to be selected, thus initiating a task execution control program.

6.3 Digit analysis program

A telephone exchange receives call connection requests by means of a register signals (dialled numbers) from subscribers or other exchanges.

In other words, the dialled number designates the call connection type and the route or terminals to be connected. The call connection type means whether a call is an intraoffice, an outgoing, a transit, a special number, or other type of call. The route is determined for outgoing and transit calls.

Therefore, it is necessary to recognise a call connection request by translating the received dialled number, and to decide upon a corresponding connection task as well as the outgoing line to be connected. This processing is called digit analysis.

The digit analysis program analyses the received dialled number, which has been received through an originating register trunk (ORT) or an incoming register trunk (IRT) and stored in the associated trunk memory, in conjunction with the originating subscriber or trunk class. As the result of this digit analysis, the program outputs an outgoing line group to be selected (called a trunk group number (TGN)), charge information for the call (called a message billing index (MBI)), and the *task number* of the corresponding connection task (expressed as a *task number* (TSKN) and a *next state number* (NSTN)).

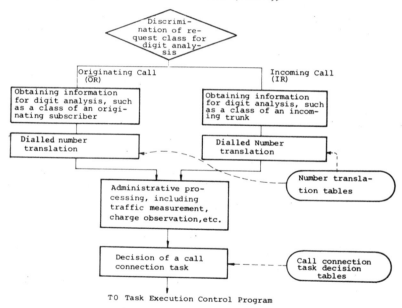

Fig. 6.6   *Digit analysis processing*

In the case of a terminating call, as a result of digit analysis, the digit analysis program activates the terminating line analysis program to recognise a terminating subscriber and analyse the call class and its state.

Furthermore, when this program recognises an abbreviated dialling number, it translates the abbreviated number into the preregistered full dialled number, using an abbreviated dialling number list stored in the system. In addition, it requests digit analysis once again.

Digit analysis processing consists of three main parts. One is dialled number translation. Another is the selection of a call connection task. The last is administrative processing, such as traffic measurement and charge observation. The processing flow is shown in Fig. 6.6.

6.3.1 Number translation

Dialled number translation is accomplished using a *number translation table*. Some number translation tables are provided separately, corresponding to call categories. For example, for originating dialled number translation, there is a general originating number translation table, a CES closed number translation table and a video originating number translation table, among others. As for terminating dialled number translation, some number translation tables are provided as well. In dialled number translation, therefore, the table which is to be used for a call must be selected first. This decision is performed using a digit block string number (DBSN) which is obtained by pretranslation and identifies the requested service class, as described previously.

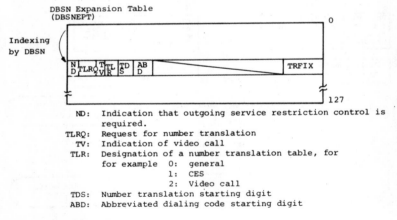

ND: Indication that outgoing service restriction control is required.
TLRQ: Request for number translation
TV: Indication of video call
TLR: Designation of a number translation table, for
   for example   0:   general
                 1:   CES
                 2:   Video call
TDS: Number translation starting digit
ABD: Abbreviated dialing code starting digit

Fig. 6.7 *DBSN expansion table*

A DBSN expansion table (DBSNEPT) is provided which gives necessary information on each DBSN for digit analysis. So, by indexing the DBSNEPT table using the obtained DBSN, the pertinent number translation table is designated. The DBSNEPT table includes not only the designation of a number translation table, but also the starting digit of the number translation, indication of a video call and some other data used in digit analysis, as shown in Fig. 6.7.

After deciding upon the number translation table, number translation is performed by indexing this table with the received dialled

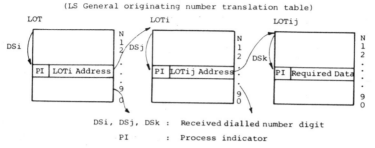

(LS General originating number translation table)

DSi, DSj, DSk : Received dialled number digit

PI : Process indicator

Fig. 6.8 *Typical number translation table example*

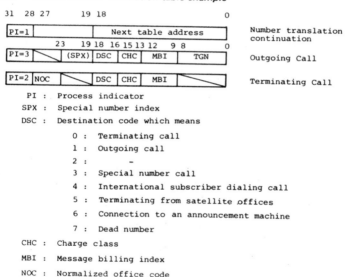

PI : Process indicator
SPX : Special number index
DSC : Destination code which means

      0 : Terminating call
      1 : Outgoing call
      2 :   –
      3 : Special number call
      4 : International subscriber dialing call
      5 : Terminating from satellite offices
      6 : Connection to an announcement machine
      7 : Dead number

CHC : Charge class
MBI : Message billing index
NOC : Normalized office code

Fig. 6.9 *Data structure examples in the number translation table*

number. The number translation table has a tree structure composed of a number of subtables. Each subtable is indexed for one digit of the received dialled number. Thus, the indexing of the number translation table by one digit after another from the starting digit will continue until the number translation is completed. A typical example of the number translation table is shown in Fig. 6.8.

Through indexing the number translation tables for each digit of the received dialled number, the required data will then be found. Some examples of the data included in the number translation table are shown in Fig. 6.9. In these data, the process indicator (PI) shows the contents of the data obtained. If number translation is not yet completed (PI = 1), the data obtained involves the next table address, and the PI indicates that the next table must be indexed for the next digit of the received dialled number. When number translation is completed, however, the data obtained depends upon the call category, including a trunk group number (TGN), a charge class (CHC), a message billing index (BMI), a call connection type (called a destination code (DSC)), and other characteristics.

Thus, as the result of number translation, the call connection request is successfully interpreted, and required data such as TGN, MBI and DSC, are obtained. In addition, the number translation tables differ according to the respective switching offices, as a matter of course. Consequently, they are generated and provided for each office individually as *office data*.

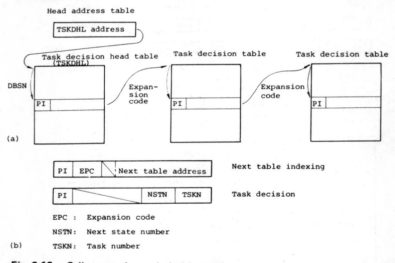

Fig. 6.10   *Call connection task decision table*
a task decision table structure
b data format

6.3.2 Call connection task decision

The decision of a call connection task is accomplished by indexing a call connection *task decision table*, shown in Fig. 6.10, with the proper data designated by an expansion code. Included in these expansion data are the digit block string number (DBSN) obtained as the result of the pretranslation, and the destination code (DSC) which means a call connection type, the special number index (SPX) by which special

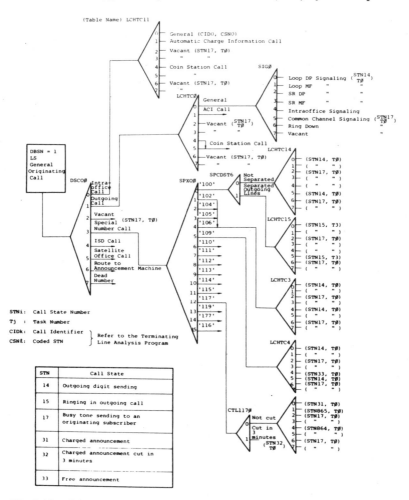

Fig. 6.11   *Call connection task decision process example*
General originating call in LS

numbers are classified, etc., that are the number translation outputs. Fig. 6.11 shows a typical example of the decision process of the call connection task.

6.3.3 Administration processing in digit analysis

The digit analysis program performs two types of administrative data collection. One is for charge determination and the other is for traffic measurement.

Charge determination, after checking whether an originating subscriber is registered by using subscriber originating class data, collects the required charge determination data and stores them in the associated charge data save area (CHGSAV) when necessary. These data include the dialled number, message billing index (MBI), charge class (CHC), etc. Moreover, the digit analysis program takes a count of various traffic measuring data, such as the total number of intraoffice calls, toll calls, special number calls, abbreviated dialling calls and international subscriber dialling calls.

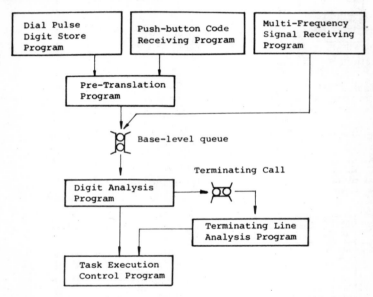

Fig. 6.12 *Relation between digit analysis program and other programs*

Digit analysis LS program (DGANLL)

This program is initiated via the base-level queue by digit-receiving programs, attaching a digit analysis request to this queue, as shown in Fig. 6.12. After choosing the call connection task, this program requests execution of this task by the task execution control program (described in the next Chapter). For a terminating call, the DGANLL program initiates the terminating line analysis program and request recognition of the terminating subscriber and analysis of the class and state.

Outgoing service restriction

In the digit analysis program, outgoing service restriction processing is arranged. If calls toward a certain destination have an extraordinary increase in number the terminating switching office will not be able to handle all of these terminating calls. This may possibly cause serious congestion in the communication network. Therefore, in such situations, it is important to put restrictions on the call connections toward this destination in the switching offices where such calls originate. This processing is called an outgoing service restriction control. Four restriction grades are provided, according to the call congestion level, and a restricted call is routed to an appropriate announcement machine, as shown in Table 6.1. There are preferential subscribers such as coin stations which are not affected by these restrictions.

Table 6.1   *Outgoing service restriction*

Restriction grade	Description	Message on announcement machine to be connected
0	Restriction on 25% of general calls	
1	Restriction on 50% of general calls	'This route is congested. Please call again after a while'
2	Restriction on 75% of general calls	
3	Restriction on all general calls	'This route is congested. Please call again from a coin station.'

Remarks 1. General calls are originated by general subscribers, except for coin stations and other preferential stations

This outgoing service restriction control is activated by registering the office code and the restriction grade by means of a teletypewriter command. The outgoing service restriction control table, shown in Fig. 6.13, is used to decide which calls should be restricted. This decision logic is described as follows. First the received dialled number of an outgoing call is compared with all registered office codes in the outgoing service restriction control table. When it coincides with one of the registered office codes, the restriction grade is then taken into account, using the outgoing service restriction control table. In this table, there are two classes of data for this purpose, the restriction grade (RN) and a control counter (CNT) which is made of 2 bits and advanced one by one whenever there is a call which has a received dialled number coincident with the registered office code. Therefore, if $RN \geqslant CNT$, then the call should be restricted and routed to an appropriate announcement machine.

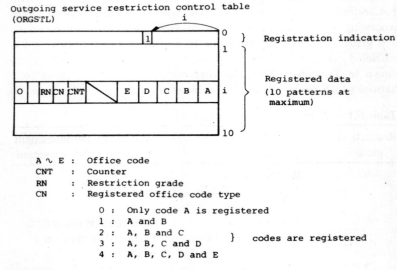

Outgoing service restriction control table (ORGSTL)

A ∿ E : Office code
CNT : Counter
RN : Restriction grade
CN : Registered office code type

    0 : Only code A is registered
    1 : A and B
    2 : A, B and C
    3 : A, B, C and D   } codes are registered
    4 : A, B, C, D and E

Fig. 6.13   *Outgoing service restriction control table*

6.4 Terminating subscriber analysis

For an intraoffice call, *terminating subscriber analysis* processes are:

   (i) to read out the terminating line translation word corresponding to the directory number from the magnetic drum

   (ii) to analyse service conditions and state, such as busy or idle, of the terminating subscriber and

   (iii) to determine the necessary task and next state number.

These processes correspond to the 'number group' function of a cross-bar exchange.

Other functions of this anlysis are malicious call tracing, designated connection and traffic observation. The means of analysing the terminating line is to search an analysis table with the input information. This is basically the same as originating subscriber analysis. The analysis table structure utilised for this anlysis is shown in Fig. 6.14. The process indicator (PI) in each analysis table designates an 'analysis macro program'.

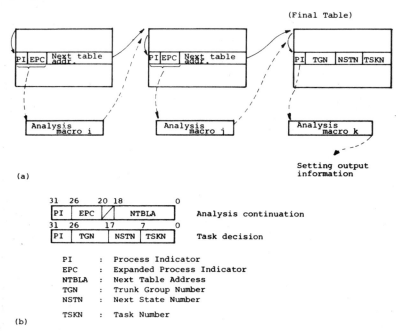

(a)

(b)

Fig. 6.14 *Table structure for terminating subscriber analysis*
a analysis table indexing method
b data structure in analysis table

Because terminating subscriber analysis is necessary for many kinds of calls and call states, the same processes appear at many branches of the expanded table for terminating subscriber anlysis. Accordingly, as illustrated in Fig. 6.14 *a*, the processes for the analysis of these conditions are designed as common program macros and then, the same processes can be treated in common. This method aims at realising a simple design with straightforward production, as well as reducing the memory required.

Next, an explanation of the analysis sequence and expansion tree structure is necessary. The order in which the analysis table is accessed needs choosing with care. First of all, the terminating line analysis table is indexed, as illustrated in Fig. 6.15, with common information for all calls, that is the 'terminating line class' such as local office subscriber or centrex subscriber (CES).

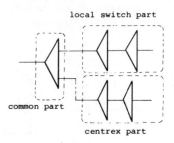

Fig. 6.15   *Analysis expansion order*

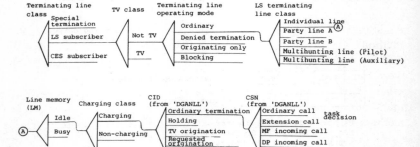

Fig. 6.16   *Example of expansion trees for terminating subscriber analysis*

Fig. 6.16 shows an example of how to determine a 'task' by way of indexing a tree with various pieces of information. The factors for analysis in Fig. 6.16 are the terminating subscriber's state and service conditions which are stored in the terminating line translation word, except for the originating side conditions which are determined from the digit analysis program.

A detailed explanation, concerning translation word configuration and the method of searching the translation word from a directory number, is covered in Section 9.9.

PBX and party-lines

In addition to the above processes, for a call to multihunting lines or a party line, an auxiliary data block, such as a multihunting list, becomes necessary to analyse a terminating subscriber. This data block is connected with a terminating line translation word. In case of multihunting line selection other directory numbers in the multihunting lines can be found by searching a multihunting list. Accordingly, the directory numbers in multihunting lines need not always be contiguous numbers.

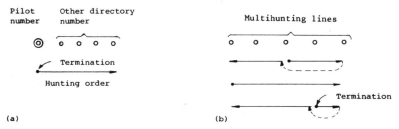

Fig. 6.17   *Multihunting lines method selection*
a sequential hunting method
b switchback method

As illustrated in Fig. 6.17, there are two multihunting line selection methods. One, (case (*a*)) is to search the multihunting list in order to find the next directory number in the multihunting lines from the first word for the call of which the dialled number is the pilot number. The other, (case (*b*)) is called the *switchback method* and is used in centrex multihunting lines. Even if a dialled number is not a pilot number, this method enables location of an idle subscriber by switch-back searching.

As the output of terminating subscriber analysis, the necessary task and next state number is obtained. In this process, since the call state is separated by a signalling system, originating side information becomes necessary for the task decision. This information is taken from a program, such as DGANLL, which activates terminating subscriber analysis. Approximately 60 macro analysis programs have been prepared. Table 6.2 shows typical examples.

Terminating subscriber analysis program (TLANL)
The terminating subscriber analysis program (TLANL) takes as input information, the terminating side information, such as directory number and abbreviated office code (NOC) and then reads out the terminating line translation word and any auxiliary blocks from the magnetic drum.

These data are used as table expansion information for decisions. This program is activated by the execution program in accordance with the indication written in a transaction memory block. This transaction is used as a 'processing request tag' and is added, as shown in Fig. 6.18,

Table 6.2   *Analysis macro (PI) classification and its function*
             (example)

PI	Expansion table format	Function
1	`PI EPC ⟋ NTBLA`	Common pattern for next table expansion. Indexing next table according to EPC.
2	`PI TGN NSTN TSKN`	Common task decision pattern. Setting necessary information, such as TGN, NSTN, TSKN to TEM (Task execution memory)
4	`PI TGN NSTN TSKN`	In addition to PI2 function, counting terminating traffic and making line memory (LM) busy.
5	`PI TGN NSTN TSKN`	Hunting PBX lines. In case there is an idle line, jump to PI4 processing. In case of all busy, busy tone connection task is obtained.
16	`PI ⟍ NTBLA`	For a call to a temporarily removed subscriber, setting the Automatic Interception System (AIS) data for announcing and then jump to PI1 processing.
EPC 2	`PI EPC ⟋ NTBLA`	Indexing a next table by a terminating line class, which is memorised in terminating translation word.
EPC 9	`PI EPC ⟋ NTBLA`	Indexing next table by LM state (idle/busy) which is read out based on terminating line equipment number (LEN). In case of busy state, counting busy connection traffic.
EPC 16	`PI EPC ⟋ NTBLA`	In case of idle state board calling, indexing next table by comparing originating tenant number result with a terminating tenant number.

in a task analysis queue (priority level: $B_1 Q_2$). As outputs of this program, the program outputs task decision information (TSKN, NSTN etc.) to the task execution memory (TEM) and activates a task execution program. In addition, for traffic measurement, it counts a predetermined traffic counter area whenever the necessity arises. Moreover, in the case of a malicious call tracing request, it sends the originating call information to a universal transaction and requests a message editing program for the output on the teletypewriter.

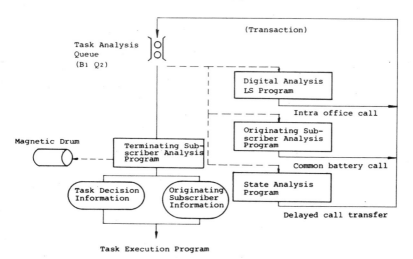

Fig. 6.18 *Terminating subscriber analysis program interface*

As explained above, the program operation is to select the analysis factors in order and to search an analysis table using the factor. Specific examples of expansion trees are shown in Fig. 6.19. This Figure shows the case of an ordinary individual subscriber.

6.5 State analysis

As described in the preceding Section, in call origination or a translation of dialled digits, an originating subscriber analysis program or a digit analysis program analyses the attributes of a subscriber or dialled digits to decide the necessary task.

On the other hand, *state analysis* is a standardised task decision method based on the concept of 'a state transition'. That is, when input signals, such as answer, disconnect and hooking, are detected in the state of the trunk connection, state analysis decides the next call state and the necessary task according to a state transition diagram.

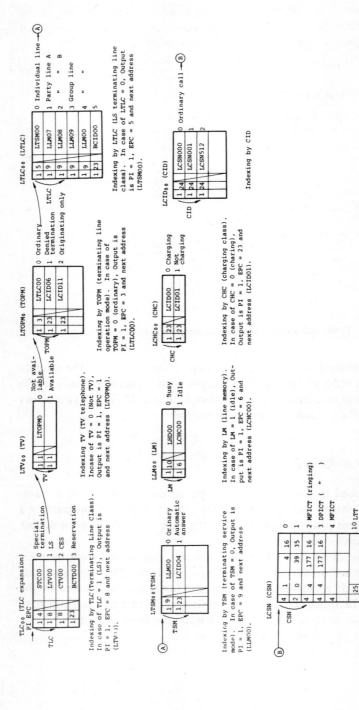

Fig. 6.19 *Example at terminating subscriber analysis expansion trees*
(ordinary individual subscriber)

State analysis decides the task by analysing the following three information areas:

(i) Call state (calling state, talking state, etc.)
(ii) Signal detection trunk (ringing trunk, speech trunk, front side, rear side, etc.)
(iii) Signal type (answer, disconnect, etc.)

These areas are given in the form of a state number (STN), a connection terminal number (CTN) and front/rear (F/R), and signal identifier (SID), respectively.

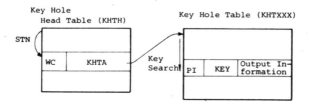

WC : Word Count (Indicating the number of Key Hole Table words)

KHTA : Key Hole Table Address

Fig. 6.20 *Analysis table searching method*

PI	KEY HOLE			NSTN	TSKN
	SID	CTN	F/R		

When next state and task number are decided.

PI	KEY HOLE			Index
	SID	CTN	F/R	

PI : Process Indicator

SID : Signal identifier

CTN : Connected Terminal Number

Fig. 6.21 *Data format in key hole table*

The state analysis may be derived directly from the state-transition diagrams of Chapter 4. Each task corresponds to a transition between states.

State analysis is based on the *table look-up method*, and uses as the keys the items such as SID, CTN and F/R. As shown in Fig. 6.20, the state analysis searches down a *key hole table* which is allocated to an individual state number by means of the input key information. Then the output information is extracted from the word, the key hole of which coincides with the input key information. Data in the key hole table are arranged as shown in Fig. 6.21. A next state number (NSTN) and a task number (TSKN) arranged in the right side are output information. If additional analysis is required, the output information shows an index according to which another analysis table should be searched. A process indicator (PI), arranged on the left, designates whether the output information is NSTN/TSKN or an index.

Table 6.3   *Example of SIDs*

SID	Abbreviation	SID content (service requests)
0	OFF	Origination, answer, blocking requests
1	ON	Disconnect Request ($\bar{A}, \bar{B}, \bar{X}$)
2	HK	Add-on, call waiting request
4	TTO	Service request after timeout ($\bar{B}_{to}$)
6	NCN	BT connection request for no-coin in coin box
8	BTR	BT connection requests
11	AT	Answer for operator assisted call
17	IF	Answer for inquiry call
.	.	.
.	.	.
.	.	.

There are approximately 100 SIDs when the attendant position keys are included, in addition to such answer and disconnect signals as described before. Table 6.3 shows typical SID signals.

State analysis program (STANLP)

The STANLP program receives a service request from the circuit, edits the input key information consisting of an STN, an SID, a CTN and an F/R, and decides the next state number and the task number. In addition, with regard to service requests requiring additional analysis related to subscriber class information, it initiates originating subscriber analysis or terminating subscriber analysis.

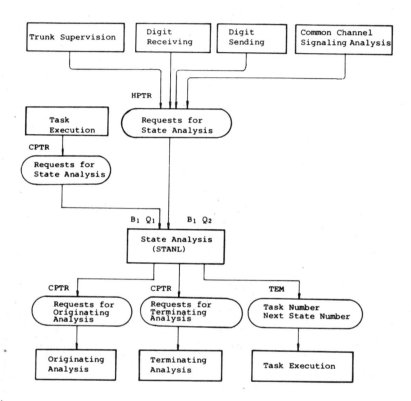

Fig. 6.22 *State analysis program assignment*

As shown in Fig. 6.22 the state analysis program is initiated by the addition of transaction memory block onto a task analysis queue $(B_1 Q_2)$ by supervisory programs. The state-analysis program executes the analysis and transfers analysis results, such as TSKN and NSTN, to the task execution control program.

An example of correspondence between state-transition diagram and key hole table is shown in Fig. 6.23.

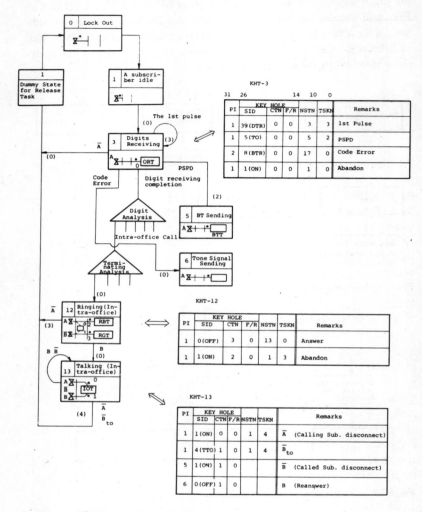

Fig. 6.23   *Correspondence between state-transition diagram and key hole table*

Chapter 7

Task execution and output programs

7.1 Philosophy of task execution

As described in the previous Chapter, a switching operation is chosen by analysing a service request class, the attributes of peripheral equipment (a subscriber line and/or trunk), and the internal state of the exchange. This switching operation is called 'a task' or 'a call processing task', which includes the selection of a trunk and a speech path, connecting them, and then executing other necessary related procedures. These task execution programs are divided into three blocks, a call processing task block, a task macro block, and a task execution control block, as shown in Fig. 7.1.

In the D-10 system, the call processing task block consists of a large number of task tables. For example, approximately 2000 task tables are provided in a local switching exchange. Each of these task tables corresponds to one of the switching operations, that is to say there is a unique task for each valid signal from each state. Each task table has a task number and it is selected by the analysis program. In general, a task is composed of a series of task macros that make up each switching operation. These task macros are expressed in interpretive code so a task macro block is made up of the interpretive programs for the task macros which form the basic procedure units for the switching operation itself.

The task execution control block selects task macros one by one from a task table, after which it interprets, and then activates the task macro interpretive programs. These programs actually execute the switching operations specified in the task table.

The introduction of the interpretive method for task macros has considerably eased the addition or change of service features compared to earlier conventional methods. This is because software modifications only require the addition or change of task macros in the task table.

7.2 Example of task table

As an example, the recorded announcement connection task for the
weather forecast will be described. As shown in Fig. 7.2, the state-
transition diagram for the weather forecast is set up by the subscriber's

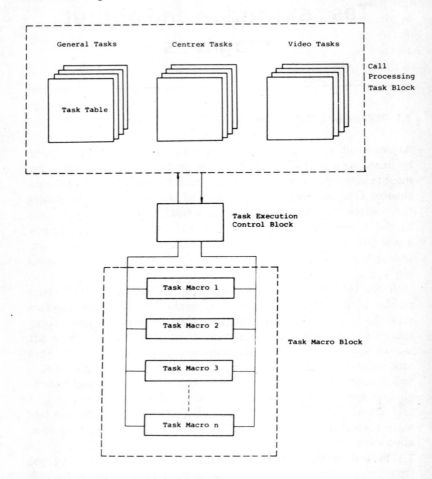

Fig. 7.1   *Task execution program configuration*

dialling 177. These dialled digits (177) are received in the state number
of 3 and in this case lead to the next state number 32. It will be seen in
Chapter 13 that the numbering scheme is based on the tasks next state.

For this example the task number is 32—0 and this is selected by the digit analysis program. An example of a task table is shown in Fig. 7.3, these are explained in more detail in Section 7.3.

The method for selecting a task table, by using a state number and a task number, is as follows (Fig. 7.4). There is a primary table indexed by the state number. This table contains the starting address of a secondary table which is indexed by a task number. The secondary table contains one entry for each task and this entry gives the starting address of the required task table.

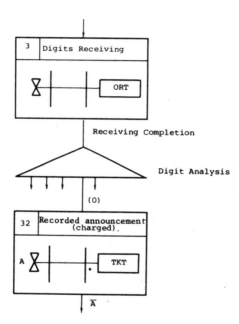

Fig. 7.2 *State-transition diagram for weather forecasting*

7.3 Task macro blocks

The task macro block is composed of the following function groups:

(*a*) *Task macro group for speech path management:* This group coordinates the functions of resource management which is the major function in the switching operation. Resources used in a call connection, such as a speech path, speech trunk and service trunk, are selected or released by means of memory operations.

MSC		FUNC	PARAMETER $(P_1, P_1, P_2, \ldots)$	Remarks
Sequence	Label			
0		LTSC	B1, B0, TEM, J0	A-TKT trunk and path hunt
1		TKSEL	B2, B2, TMR, J1	TMR register hunt
2		TRMTRM	B0, B1, CLTE	CLS transfer
3		TEMTRM	BC-CHCMBI, B1, TOGM-CHCMBI	CHCMBI transfer
4		LINKA	B1, B2, B0, , , 3	
5		TKTE	B1, , S0, T0	
6		ORTE	B0, , S2, T3	
7		JOBEX		
8		MCLA	B0, B0	Billing processing for answer time
9		TMTS	B2, R	PSPD timer reset
10		TQCTL	B1, ATCH, TKT, TK	TMT timer reset
11		LNR	B2, TI, RSTRT, N	A-ORT trunk and path release
12		SMCU	B0, EON	TKTSM data set
13		LINKC	2	
14		ENDT		
15	J1	LNR	B1, TI, NEF, N	
16	J0	SORL	STANL, BLK0	

Fig. 7.3   *Task table example (recorded announcement task)*

(b) *Task macro group for speech path order editing:* This group edits the control orders for speech path control equipment corresponding to the memory operation in the speech path management, as described above.

(c) *Task macro group for bill processing:* This group collects billing information, such as message rate (based on the duration time and the message billing index) and counts it up in the service-meter. In addition to this, in response to requests from subscribers concerning billing, detailed billing information can be collected for verification.

(*d*) *Task macro group for traffic measurement:* This group counts up the number of calls for every call category using an individual task. This task macro group, in addition to other traffic measurement programs, makes up the total traffic measurement system in the switching systems.

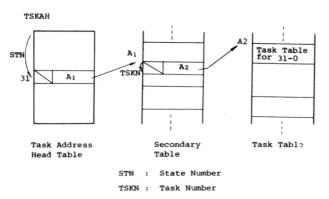

STN : State Number

TSKN : Task Number

Fig. 7.4 *Task table selection*

(*e*) *Task macro group for translation or conversion:* This group translates one equipment number to another, for example, a trunk number (TN) to a network equipment number (NEN) or two-wire voice circuit number to a four-wire video circuit number.

(*f*) *Task macro group for data set or data transfer:* This group sets call control data, such as call state number, supervisory state and system output, into a designated memory area and then transfers the data from one area to another.

(*g*) *Task macro group for task control:* This group controls the end of task, transfer of control, and waiting procedures of a task.

Form of task macro

Thus task macros can be defined as a software instruction of a very high level while a task table is made up of an assembly of task macros which are interpreted at task execution time. In other words, the task macro block is an assembly of interpretive routines corresponding to each task macro. There are approximately 150 task macros, samples of which are shown in Fig. 7.5.

Fig. 7.5 also shows, the format of each task macro. Eight bits, from the 31st to the 24th bit, are used as a function name, i.e. the task macro name. The remaining bits below the 23rd bit are used as the

Task Macro Name	Format	Function Outline

Line to Trunk Selection and Connection	`31  24  20  16   7    0`
	 `[ LTSC | Bi | Bj | TGN | α ]`
	
	 Bi, Bj: Block number in working area for the task execution (TEM)
	
	 TGN : Trunk Group Number to select a trunk
	
	 α : Macro Step Count (MSC) to branch in case of trunk busy
		Selecting a trunk in accordance with TGN, registering the selected trunk number and the corresponding trunk memory address into Bi, selecting a speech path between the network equipment number (NEN) for the selected trunk and the line equipment number (LEN) in Bj, and registering the results into Bi and the relevant trunk memory.

Trunk Selection	`31  24  20  16        0` `[ TKSEL | Bi | Bj | TGN | α ]`	Selecting a trunk in accordance with TGN, registering the selected trunk number and the corresponding trunk memory address in Bi, and registering the network equipment number in Bj. This macro is used for timer register selection as well as for trunk selection.

Outgoing Trunk (OGT) Editing	`31  24  20  16  10   6`
	 `[ OGTE | Bi | Bj | Sk | Tℓ | ▧ ]`
	
	 Sk: Trunk State before transition
	
	 Tℓ: Transition task number
		Editing connection or disconnection order for a speech path between an OGT and an ICT/a subscriber line, and trunk relay control order.

Fig. 7.5 *Example of task macros*

parameter part for each task macro. The actual value of the parameter part is set in each task table.

Task macros LTSC (line-to-trunk selection and connection), TKSEL (trunk selection), etc., can be used in most task tables. A general flow-chart of an interpretive routine for LTSC macro is shown in Fig. 7.6.

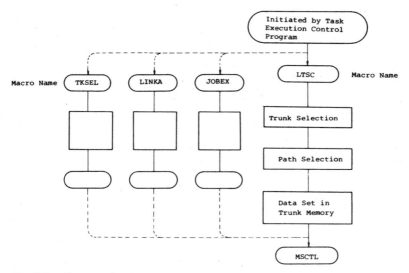

Fig. 7.6   *Essence of task macros*

7.4 Task execution control program (TEXCTL)

This program searches the selected task table and selects task macros from the task table one by one. For each task macro it initiates a rel-evant interpretive routine to complete the necessary switching operation. The function of the task execution control program consists of the following four parts.

(i) *Selection of a task table:* The selection of the task table is determined by the task number given by the analysis programs. This is done by searching the task address table as described above. There are so many task tables in the system that a large memory area is necess-ary for these tables. Some for instance, intraoffice connection tasks and incoming/outgoing connection tasks (which are frequently ex-ecuted) are allocated in the main memory equipment for faster access. However, other tasks are usually allocated in the magnetic-drum mem-ory to achieve economy. When the required task table is allocated in the magnetic drum memory, it is read out to a common area in the main memory by the task execution control program. This common area is used by every task table allocated in the magnetic drum memory. This method is called *'Task overlay control'*.

(ii) *Transaction memory block hunting:* There are different types of transaction memory blocks required at different phases of the task execution. The task execution control program compares the transaction memory block class (which is controlled by analysis programs) with the transaction class that is needed for the task execution (written in the task address table). When a new transaction memory block is necessary for the task execution, this program then hunts for a new block and transfers the data from an old transaction memory block into the new block.

(iii) *Speech path information setting:* Before task execution can occur, all the speech path information contained in the linked trunk records must be copied into a task execution memory (TEM).

(iv) *Macro step control:* This part retrieves task macros consecutively one by one in accordance with their arrangement in the task table, interprets them, and then initiates the relevant interpretive routines. A macro step counter is provided to indicate the task macro to be executed next.

A process flowchart of the task execution control program is shown in Fig. 7.7. The main procedure of a switching operation is to connect a speech path. For this purpose, the task execution program selects a trunk and a speech path, after which it edits the speech path control order and sets up other data as required by the task procedures. However, sending the control order to the speech path controller equipment (SP controller) and operating the switch or the trunk are not performed by the task execution program. This is because the electromechanical operation takes more operating time than the program execution. Consequently, the task execution is interrupted when the speech path control order is sent (which is executed by another program). These speech path control orders (SP orders) are loaded into a speech path transaction memory block (SP transaction) and attached to the SP transaction queue, from which the output processing program retrieves the SP orders to be sent to the SP controller.

When the speech path control program, which is one of the output processing programs, has finished sending SP orders to the SP controller, it attaches the SP transaction to the internal processing queue $(B_1 Q_1)$. This transaction is again retrieved, to initiate the task execution control program, which restarts the execution of the remaining part of the task table (from the macro indicated by the macro step counter). The remaining parts of the task table generally include the freeing of the trunk or the path (which has just been released hardware-

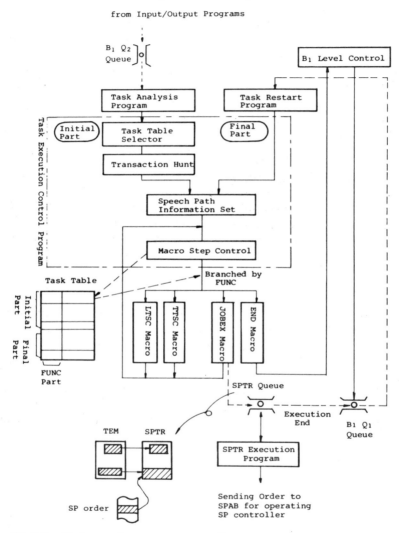

Fig. 7.7 *Task execution program process flow*

wise by the speech path control program), update of a supervisory memory, storage of a new state number into the trunk memories, and release of the SP transaction memory block.

The method for editing of the SP orders is shown in Fig. 7.8. These SP orders, which are control commands for the SP controller, are edited by the task macros provided for each class of trunk. They include the

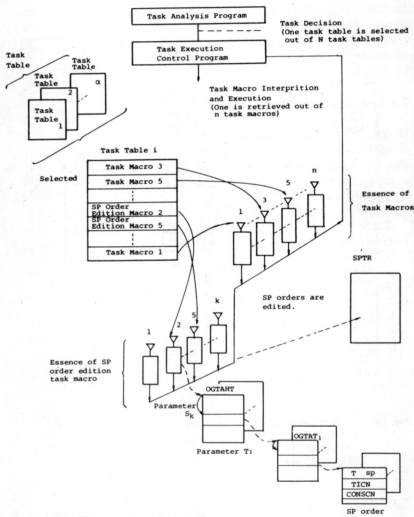

Fig. 7.8   *SP transaction editing outline*

commands that connect the speech path, execute the network continuity test and drive the trunk relays. Required SP orders for one state transition are selected by task macros, such as OGTE and ICTE, and their parameters in the task table. They are loaded into the SP transaction memory block (Fig. 7.8).

Thus, it may be seen that an individual switching operation unit is represented by each task macro, a type of higher level language, to facilitate programming. In addition to his, all the jobs required for the state transition are described by the task table, and are classified according to the state number. This approach achieves clearness with respect to the interface in the system.

7.5 Speech-path equipment control

Output processing is required for device control in the speech-path subsystem, such as a crossbar switch and a relay setting and/or resetting. In addition, the output processing program includes a digits-sending program, a charging pulse sending control program, and some other programs. This Section deals with the speech-path equipment control and the next with the remaining functions.

The speech path equipment control is divided into a network control (a small crossbar switch control) and a relay control.

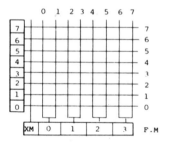

Fig. 7.9   *8 × 8 mechanical latching type cross bar switch*
RM reset magnet
XM crosspoint magnet
FM finger magnet

7.5.1 Network control

The D-10 ESS has adopted an 8 × 8 mechanical latching type crossbar switch, which has 8 levels in vertical and horizontal sides, respectively, as shown in Fig. 7.9. There is a reset magnet (RM) at each vertical level. On the horizontal side, there are a cross point magnet (XM), which operates only when odd levels are selected and four finger magnets

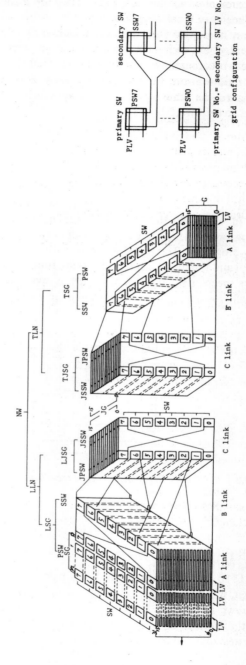

Fig. 7.10   *Network configuration*

(FM), each of which controls a set of two levels (one is an odd level and the other is an even one). Horizontal levels are selected by the combination of these two (XM and FM) magnets.

Fig. 7.10 shows a network configuration using this crossbar switch. The network consists of a 4-stage line link network (LLN) and a 4-stage trunk link network (TLN). The information required for controlling this crossbar switch is:

(*a*) Equipment selection information
(*b*) Primary switch input level (PLV)
(*c*) Secondary switch output level (JSLV)
(*d*) Primary switch number (PSW)
(*e*) Secondary switch number (JSSW)
(*f*) Grid number (G)
(*g*) Order (connection or disconnection)

All of this information is stored in an SP transaction memory block (SPTR).

An SPTR execution program, which will be explained later, sends the information shown in Table 7.1 to a speech-path address bus (SPAB). The information in Table 7.1 is generated from the information in an SP transaction memory block.

A switch controller (SC) receives this information and controls a selected RM, XM and FM by separating the information, as shown in Fig. 7.11. Now, according to the above operation, the SC can drive a selected cross point in a crossbar switch. This means that an SC can control the connection and the disconnection of a speech-path.

7.5.2 *Relay control by relay controller*

As an RC needs some operate waiting time, relay control by an RC can be applied to a relay which does not require a highly accurate operating time, as compared with a relay that is controlled by a signal distributor (SD).

Examples of low accuracy timing relays are the S and T relays used for changing the conditions in a trunk circuit. The control by an RC uses a similar control method to the network. In other words, when the SPTR execution program sends the information shown in Table 7.2 to SPAB, information is generated from the RC order in the SP transaction edited by the internal processing. This information is expanded by the decoder and the path selection relay (PSR) circuit shown in Fig. 7.12. Then, the RC sets or resets a relay in a selected point whose physical location is given by the bit position $C_9 - C_0$.

Table 7.1 *SPAB information format*

Bit fields (bits 33–18):
- Bit 33 = S
- Bit 32 = P
- Bits 31–28 = Main equipment number
- Bits 27–21 = Internal equipment number
- Bits 20–18 = (blank)

Data fields (bits 17–0):

Row	17	16	15	14	13	12	11	10	9	8	7	6	5	4	3	2	1	0
L°SC 1st-order							M_2	M_1	J_3	J_2	J_1	J_0	Y_5	Y_4	Y_3	Y_2	Y_1	Y_0
field							LN		JG				JSSW			JSLV		
L°SC 2nd-order	O_2	O_1	O_0	X_{14}	X_{13}	X_{12}	X_{11}	X_{10}	X_9	X_8	X_7	X_6	X_5	X_4	X_3	X_2	X_1	X_0
field	Order			N		SG			G				PSW			PLV		
T°SC 1st-order							M_2	M_1	J_3	J_2	J_1	J_0	Y_5	Y_4	Y_3	Y_2	Y_1	Y_0
field							LN		JG				JSSW			JSLV		
T°SC 2nd-order	O_2	O_1	O_0	0	0	0	0	0	Z_9	Z_8	Z_7	Z_6	Z_5	Z_4	Z_3	Z_2	Z_1	Z_0
field	Order			all '0'					G				PSW			PLV		

(The 2nd-order rows repeat the S, P, Main equipment number and Internal equipment number columns — shown by ditto marks " — from the 1st-order rows.)

° LSC: Line link network switch controller   ° TSC: Trunk link network switch controller

Table 7.2 *SPAB information format*

Bit fields (bits 33–18):
- Bit 33 = S
- Bit 32 = P
- Bits 31–28 = Main equipment number
- Bits 27–21 = Internal equipment number

Data fields (bits 12–0):

Row	12	11	10	9	8	7	6	5	4	3	2	1	0
RC	O_1	O_0	C_{10}	C_9	C_8	C_7	C_6	C_5	C_4	C_3	C_2	C_1	C_0
field	Order		S/T	X			Y			L			

$O_1 O_0$: Set/Reset C_{10} : S/T relay distinction $C_9 \sim C_0$: Relay accommodated point

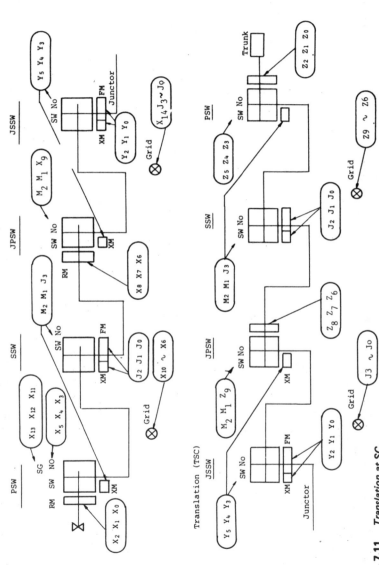

Fig. 7.11 *Translation at SC*

SPTR execution program (SPTREX)

The small crossbar switch control and the relay control, which are parts of the speech-path subsystem control, need a mechanical operation time of about 16 ms after receiving an order. Accordingly, a controller is blocked for 16 ms after receiving an order. This is why the SC or RC uses an electromechanical device, called a path selection relay (PSR), and controls a switch or a relay by using a sequence of operations. For these reasons, the sending of an SP order is controlled by a single program (called SPTR execution program) which is used for the purpose of process standardisation. This program is similar to the channel used in the input-output subsystem.

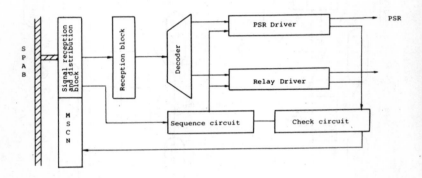

Fig. 7.12   *Information reception from SPAB, expansion and relay drive circuit*

Data is input to SPTREX by adding an SP transaction memory block to the SP transaction active chain (SPTRACT). In these transactions, SP orders, such as switch control orders and relay control orders, are edited by a task (initial task) and by other programs in the call processing. As shown in Fig. 7.13, several SP orders may be entered into these transactions and are executed consecutively by the SPTREX. When the SP order is an equipment drive order, the order is sent to the SPAB in the information format which was described above.

The process in the SPTREX is executed according to the following sequences as shown in Fig. 7.14:

(i) Obtain a transaction memory block from the SPTRACT.

(ii) Determine the order to be executed by indexing with a Pointer (PNT) within the transaction.

(iii) Check the designated equipment (RC or SC) busy or idle state, unless the selected order is an 'end order'.

(iv) In case of an idle state, edit the order in the transaction memory block to the format shown in Tables 7.1 and 7.2 and then send it to the SPAB.

(v) Update the PNT for the next process.

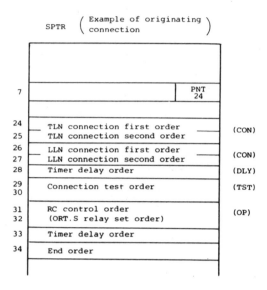

Fig. 7.13 *Order example in SPTR*

Relay control by signal distributor (SD)

The signal distributor can request the operation or release of a relay within the machine cycle of the processor as each point fed from SD has its own electronic memory element. Unlike the RC an SD operation does not need an operation waiting time. Accordingly, the SD controls relays for which the delay in operating time is unacceptable, for example, a digit-sending relay or a charging pulse sending relay.

The central control equipment (CC) sends relay control information in a special pattern, whereupon the SD automatically receives this pattern as 16 flip-flops (FF) of information. Since each of the FFs corresponds to a relay driver device, the relay control of the SD can then execute with 16 points in parallel.

One SD consists of 16 points × 8 rows = 128 points and 16 points can be controlled at a time with information formatted as shown in Table 7.3. In this table, $R_3 - R_0$ means a row of selected equipment and

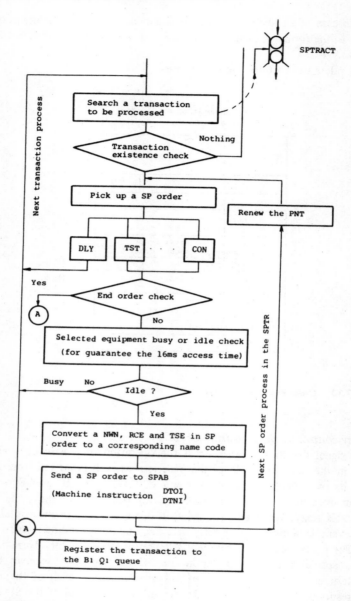

Fig. 7.14   *SPTREX process outline*

Table 7.3 *SPAB information format*

SD	Bit																																
	33	32	31	30	29	28	27	26	25	24	23	22	21	20	19	18	17	16	15	14	13	12	11	10	9	8	7	6	5	4	3	2	1	0
S	P													R_3	R_2	R_1	R_0	P_{15}	P_{14}	P_{13}	P_{12}	P_{11}	P_{10}	P_9	P_8	P_7	P_6	P_5	P_4	P_3	P_2	P_1	P_0

Main equipment number — bits 31–27
Internal equipment number — bits 26–20
Row — bits 19–16
Pattern — bits 15–0

$P_{15}-P_0$ is a set of 16 relay points. Fig. 7.15 shows the reception and expansion of the information from the SPAB.

Since the SD controls 16 points simultaneously, all the orders specified by $P_{15}-P_0$ must be sent even if only one point is necessary to be controlled. For example, in Fig. 7.16 *a* when it is only necessary to control a P_8 relay, all the orders shown in Fig. 7.16 *b* must be sent. Thus, state (*a*) must have been memorized before sending the order (*b*).

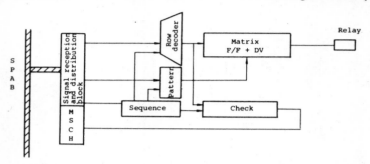

Fig. 7.15   *Information reception from SPAB and expansion*

```
P₁₅                P₈              P₀
  1 0 1 1 0 0 0 1 0 0 1 1 1 0 0 1  ◂── (a) Relay state before sending order
  1 0 1 1 0 0 0 1 1 0 1 1 1 0 0 1  ◂── (b) Order
```

Fig. 7.16   *Example of P_8 relay reset order*

7.6 Digit sending

For an outgoing call it is necessary to send the required digits of the dialled number to a corresponding exchange. This digit-sending is performed by a dial pulse digit-sending program (DPSNSP) or a multi-frequency digit sending program (MFSNDP). These are used in the call connection state of 'outgoing digit sending', in which an outgoing trunk (OGT) is connected with an outgoing sender trunk (OST) appropriate to the OGT signalling system.

The digits to be sent are stored in the OST trunk memory (OSM) and sending is under the control of data stored in either a dial pulse supervisory memory (DPOST-SM) or an MF supervisory memory (MFOST-SM). These supervisory memories each control a number of senders in a manner similar to the supervisory memories used for signalling receivers (Chapter 4). For instance, the data stored in the DPOST supervisory memory is shown in Fig. 7.17. There are 9 bits of information for each OST. The individual bits for up to 256 OSTs are stored in up to 8 consecutive 32-bit words.

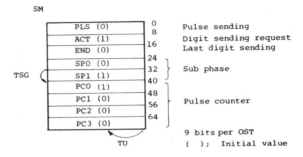

Fig. 7.17 *Dial pulse outgoing sender trunk supervisory memory (DPOST-SM)*

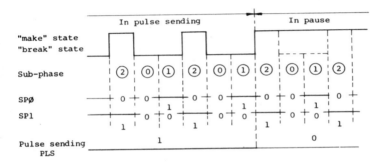

Sub-phase Pulse sending	⓪ → ①	① → ②	② → ⓪
In pulse sending (PLS = 1)	No operation	Resetting the SD	Setting the SD counting down the pulse counter
In pause (PLS = 0)	No operation	No operation	Counting down the pulse counter

Fig. 7.18 *Dial pulse sending method*

7.6.1 Dial pulse digit-sending program (DPSNDSP)

The dial pulse digit-sending program, which is initiated every 32 ms examines the DPOST supervisory memory of Fig. 7.17, and starts the digit-sending processing for those DPOSTs for which the digit sending requests (ACT bits) are set.

The control method is based on the use of three subphases 0, 1 and

2 specified by two bits SP0, SP1. The subphase is advanced at each 32 ms activation and, as shown in Fig. 7.18, the SD is reset when the subphase moves from subphase 1 to 1 and set at the transition from 2 to 0.

The number of pulses sent is controlled by the pulse sending bit (PLS) in the SM. This PLS bit is used as a gate for a sequence of pulses that are generated at regular intervals. Therefore, the gate opening interval controls the number of sending pulses.

Thus the SD setting order is output when the subphase is 2 and

$$(ACT) \wedge (PLS) \wedge (SP1) = 1,$$

while the SD resetting order is output when the subphase is 1 and

$$(ACT) \wedge (PLS) \wedge (SP0) = 1,$$

where the ACT bit represents the digit sending request of the corresponding OST.

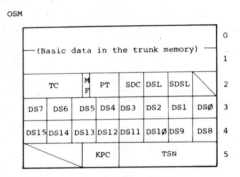

OSM

TC	MF	PT	SDC	DSL	SDSL		2
DS7	DS6	DS5	DS4	DS3	DS2	DS1	DS0	3
DS15	DS14	DS13	DS12	DS11	DS10	DS9	DS8	4
		KPC		TSN			5

DSL   :   Digit sending length

SDC   :   Sending start digit

DSi   :   Sending Digits
(i=0∿15)

MF   :   Dial pulse/Multi-frequency = 0/1

TSN   :   Trunk scanner number for the supervision
          of the acknowledgement signal

Fig. 7.19   *Outgoing sender trunk memory (OSM)*

The digits to be sent are stored in the OGT trunk memory (OSM), as shown in Fig. 7.19. The digit that should be sent is transferred and set in the *pulse counter* in the SM (PC0–PC3). This pulse counter is decremented by one every 96 ms (i.e. three 32 ms subphase intervals), while the PLS bit stays on until the pulse counter becomes zero. After completion of a digit transmission, the next digit is set in the pulse counter from the OSM, and the dial pulse sending continues as before. The pulse counter is also used for controlling the interdigit-pause timing and the post-pause timing. For example, the interdigit-pause is produced by counting down of the pulse counter six times ($96 \times 6 = 576$ ms). When this occurs, the SD control is not performed as it is not in the pulse sending state (PLS = 0).

7.6.2 Multifrequency digit-sending program (MFSNDP)

The multifrequency digit-sending program performs digit-sending processing by controlling the signal distributor (SD), based on the information set in the multifrequency otgoing sender trunk supervisory memory (MFOST-SM) and the MFOST trunk memory (OSM), in much the same way as in the dial pulse digit sending. However, digits sent by the MFSNDP are multifrequency signals (MF) coded as a combination of 2 out of 6 frequencies, instead of a sequence of pulses.

The MFSNDP program is initiated every 52 ms, and examines the MFOST supervisory memories, the format of which is shown in Fig. 7.20. It then processes digit sending for those MFOSTs, for which the digit sending requests (ACT bits) are set.

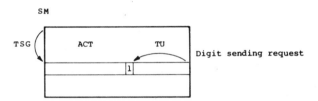

Fig. 7.20 *Multifrequency outgoing sender trunk supervisory memory (MFOST-SM)*

The processing procedure in MF digit sending is indicated by the program tag (PT) in the OSM, as shown in Fig. 7.21. First, the PT is set at zero. This means that the OST is in the waiting state for the backward seizure acknowledgement signal (OFF signal). After detecting the OFF signal, the MFSNDP sets PT = 1 and instructs the SD to send the start of pulsing signal (KP signal). These controlled SD points are selected, on the basis of the frequency combination pattern that corresponds to the sending digit, as shown in Fig. 7.22. After transmission of the KP signal, the OST is in the state of waiting for the backward KP acknowledgement signal (ON signal) (PT = 1). When the ON signal is detected, the PT is set at 2 and a 156 ms delay timing is activated.

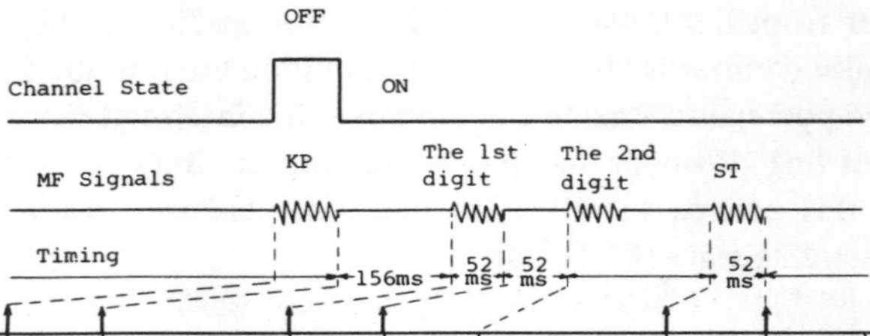

PT	0	1	2	3	4	3 ∿ 4	5	6	7
State	Waiting for OFF Signal	Waiting for ON Signal	Delay Timing	Digit Sending	Digit Sending Stop	Repeated Digit Sending Procedure	ST Signal Sending	ST Signal Sending Stop	End of Digit Sending

⟶ Processing procedure

Fig. 7.21 *MF digit-sending procedure*

SP point / Code	K	7	4	2	1	0
1					1	1
2				1		1
3				1	1	
4			1			1
5			1		1	
6			1	1		
7		1				1
8		1			1	
9		1		1		
10		1	1			
KP	1			1		
ST	1				1	

Fig. 7.22 *MF signals and corresponding SD points*

After this timing has occurred, the first digit is sent by setting the SD according to the frequency combination pattern (PT = 3), and then 52 ms later resetting the SD (PT = 4). Thus the digits have been transmitted, the end of pulsing signal (ST signal) is sent.

Metering pulse sending

In Japanese local electronic switching systems, the *decentralised charging method* is employed, rather than the use of mechanical charging meters operated by metering pulses that are generated by trunk exchanges. In this charging method, the charging meter memory, which is allocated in the drum memory, is used to accumulate and register the message rates. These rates are calculated by dividing the conversation duration (the conversation ending time minus the conversation starting time) by the charging unit time during program processing.

However, the meter pulse sending function is still required in electronic switching systems for collecting coins at coin-stations, or for charging for calls at satellite crossbar or step-by-step exchanges, etc. Therefore, metering pulse sending is necessary for output processing.

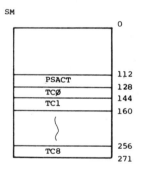

PSACT: Active indication for
         charging supervision

TCØ
 ?   : Charging timing counter
TC8

Fig. 7.23   *Charging trunk supervisory memory*

This metering pulse sending is performed in the following way. First, the charging time counter is provided in the supervisory memory of the charging trunks, as shown in Fig. 7.23. It is decremented every 500 ms. When the charging time counter becomes zero, the metering pulse is sent to the preceding exchange or coin-station by controlling the corresponding trunk relay point. In such a processing, much of the processing capacity is required for the timing supervision and the relay control for many charging trunks. However, delay in metering pulse sending should be reduced as much as possible. To solve these problems, timing supervision is performed on the basis of group processing in a similar fashion to that described above, and the signal distributor (SD) control method is utilised for relay control.

Chapter 8

Fault processing

Call processing has been described so far. This Section describes fault processing which maintains call processing continuity, even in the presence of malfunctions.

A telephone exchange is required to provide continuous switching operation and stable service over a long period of time. It is never possible to construct a totally reliable hardware and software system so any system must include the means to detect and remove a trouble and to recover normal operation of the system as soon as possible.

To meet these objectives, the electronic switching system provides both hardware and software with countermeasures against faults. Hardware features include a redundancy arrangement, in which commonly used equipment is provided with a standby unit. A particular circuit to detect faults is added to each unit. Software features automatically identify the faulty unit, switch the load over to a standby unit and re-start the switching operation quickly. The software also furnishes a fault message to the maintenance engineer. In addition, a diagnosis program is provided, which tests an isolated unit and furnishes the necessary information for locating a fault (see Chapter 9).

8.1 Fault processing outline

The possible faults encountered with an electronic switching system may include trouble caused by a program error as well as a fault in terminal equipment, such as a trunk or a network, and in common equipment, such as central control, memory and speech path control equipment. The following paragraphs explain how the electronic switching system copes with such faults.

For common equipment, check circuits are provided at important positions to check for a trouble at the moment the equipment is used. When a fault is detected, the faulty subsystem is switched out of service (under program control) and processing continued. This is the simplest case and it assumes that normal service is restored immediately after the reconfiguration. It is a problem, however, when the program control itself fails due to a critical fault in the central control or memory or when program control is lost and program confusion takes place due to a program bug in a function which is seldom used. To cope with such a trouble, the hardware clock (called a watchdog or fault detection timer) is initialised at given intervals by the program during normal operation times. If the program control is lost, the timer will indicate timeout, thereby detecting a trouble in the system. In such a case, it is difficult to get the system back where it was, since the immediately preceding status of the program or equipment is unkown. For this reason, *the emergency action control circuit* is actuated upon the detection of a trouble, this circuit establishes the minimum working equipment subsystem consisting of central control and memory. Then, the configuration is gradually expanded under program control until the switching operation is enabled.

Furthermore a trouble may occur owing to malfunction of the fault detection circuit, or some unforeseeable trouble may exist. Even when a decision cannot be made for recovery processing, in the event of such a trouble, *restart processing* is performed with the above-mentioned emergency action control circuit, thereby providing the system with a self-recovering function.

A program is an assembly of logical steps and exists for a proper logical structure. In handling a trouble, such as a fault, however, processing logic may or may not be constructed in such a manner as to be able to handle the trouble. Also, if the stored data contents are erroneous, for some reason, in the course of the program execution, the processing logic may become unsound. This will result in a deadlock as to which processing is to be taken next. Of course, such irregular phenomena will very rarely occur. Even in this situation, however, the call processing must not be stopped. When the program cannot determine the processing, the emergency action control circuit is initiated to resume call processing. When it can re-establish processing, control is returned to a specified program for resumption of call processing.

Fig. 8.1 shows the fault processing flow.

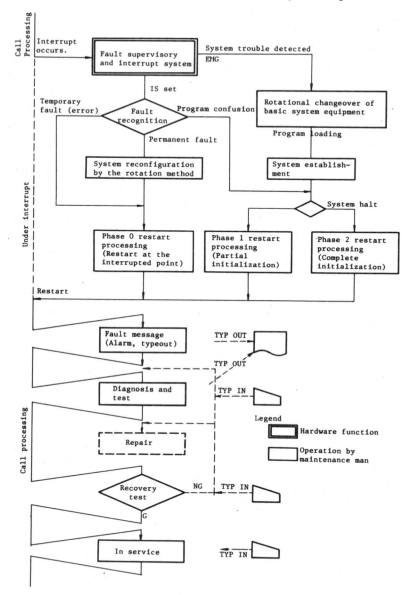

Fig. 8.1   *Fault processing flow*

8.2 Fault processing methods

To detect a trouble in the process of the switching operation, the terminal equipment such as a speech path switch and a trunk are checked for normalcy by a continuity test or false connection ground test. Common control equipment, such as central control, memory and speech path control equipment, are checked by hardware and software, as follows.

8.2.1 Fault detection by hardware

Each unit is provided with various check circuits to check normalcy of the results each time the unit is operated. When a trouble is detected, the following methods are available to report it to software.

(*a*) *Class A interrupt:* For faults with a high degree of urgency, a class A interrupt source (AIS) flip-flop is set on. Then, an interrupt returning the control address of central control to a predetermined fixed address will take place, reporting the fault to the program. Classification of these interrupt sources (IS) is shown in Table 8.1

Table 8.1 *Class A interrupt source classification*

IS classification	interrupt sources	
0	Manual clear start (manual operation at maintenance console)	
1	Emergency action control circuit initiation	
2 – 7	Central control trouble	
8 – 12	Memory trouble	Trouble in the central processing subsystem
13 – 15	Illegal code etc.	
16 – 17	Equipment trouble, in the speech path subsystem	
18, 20 – 27	Equipment trouble in the input output subsystem	

(*b*) *Status check:* When there is a trouble that will not affect program control itself, such as a trouble in the speech path or input/output subsystem equipment, this is detected when it is operated autonomously by orders from central control. For such equipment, the main program regularly checks the status indicator.

(*c*) *Initiation of emergency action control circuit:* If the fault detected by hardware is such that program control itself becomes doubtful, the above methods are not effective. In this case, the emergency action control circuit is initiated.

This kind of fault includes a time-out of the fault detection timer (TF), an irregular central control operation mode* and a central control clock stop.

(*d*) *External supervisory circuit:* This circuit is provided separately from the call processing system to check the overall function by evaluating the switching operation objectively from the outside. It generally operates by making test calls and checking for return of dial tone. When a trouble is detected by this circuit, the emergency action control circuit will then be initiated.

8.2.2 Fault detections by program

An irregular state detected by the program includes program control disorder and data contents inconsistency. For instance, program control disorder detection includes:

(*a*) *Endless loop check:* When a program control falls into disorder and the execution of a program is repeated endlessly, the program will be in a *maze*. If this occurs at anything but the highest interrupt level it will be detected by a program. When program operation is normal, the program is executed in various program levels. If control is not transferred from one level to another level within a specified period of time, however, it will be judged to be the occurrence of an endless loop.

(*b*) *Logical trouble detection:* If a table is referred to by indexing that does not exist logically, the action will be judged to be a trouble.

Data contents inconsistency detection include:

(i) *Detection of a memory block reserved for a long time:* If a memory block (such as transaction memory block) used in common pool is reserved for an extremely long time, the trouble is detected and the information will be placed out on the teletypewriter unit to give the fault message to the maintenance engineer.

(ii) *Nonmatching duplicate data:* Duplicate data on the magnetic drum are checked periodically to guard against memory destruction.

---

* This mode specifies which of two duplicate central controls is active and can control the equipment configuration. One is active and the other is standby.

(iii) *Long time trunk or link reservation:* If a trunk or a link is reserved for an extremely long time, this fact is detected and the information will be typed out to give the maintenance engineer the fault
message.

Error counters
An equipment trouble detected by hardware does not require immediate fault processing when it occurs due to noise effects or when the
trouble is intermittent. To discriminate between such temporary faults
(called *errors*) and permanent faults, an error counter is activated each
time a fault interrupt occurs. When the counter exceeds a predetermined value, the program will judge the state to be a permanent fault
and change the load on faulty equipment over to the standby equipment. This method is referred to as *an error-counter method*, which is
taken into consideration to prevent the system from being affected by
mere noise.

The error counter is cleared for each specified period of time. If an
intermittent fault occurs frequently, owing to deterioration in equip-.
ment components, the counter value will rise suddenly. Therefore, the
fault will be handled similarly to a permanent fault. If the fault is
originally a permanent fault, the error counter will exceed the predetermined value immediately. The error counter method flow is shown
in Fig. 8.2.

8.3 Reconfiguration

As described in Chapter 1, the various pieces of equipment, composing
the electronic switching system, are classified into three categories: a
central processing subsystem (central control, memory and data channel), an input ouput system (multiplexer channel, magnetic drum and
teletypewriter unit) and a speech path subsystem (signal receiver-
distributor, switch controller, etc.). The electronic switching system is
operated by a combination of these units together with the programs.
When a fault is detected by one of the fault-detection methods described above, it is generally easy to identify the faulty unit. However,
an ordinary fault recognition method may lead to misjudgement, depending on a faulty part or failure symptom. It is practically impossible
to guard against all possible conditions for preventing such misjudgement, since the combinations of these conditions are almost infinite in
number. This is the major difficulty in the design of a fault-processing
program.

To exclude such indefinite conditions, a cyclic changeover method, so-called *rotation method*, has been adopted for recognition of a faulty unit. This is a very straightforward technique. First, the fault is localised to a major equipment subsystem. Then, the individual subsystems in the major subsystem are switched over to standby condition, one after another, and the processing resumed on each occasion. When no fault appears, the immediately preceding equipment, replaced by the standby equipment, will be determined to be faulty.

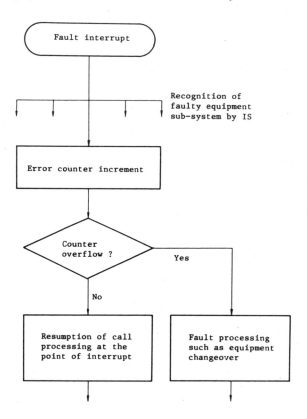

Fig. 8.2   *Error counter method*

Fig. 8.3 illustrates the structure of fault processing performed by removal of the faulty equipment until the switching operation is restored through the configuration of a normal active system. As shown in this flow, if the error counter is below a predetermined value, the switching operation is resumed at the interrupted point (through the

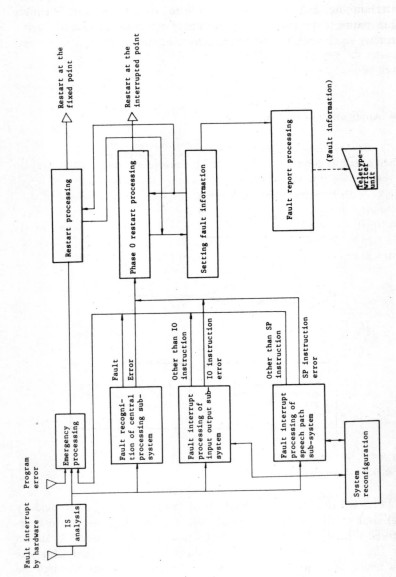

Fig. 8.3   *Fault processing structure*

error route) even when a fault is detected by the fault detection circuit. With a permanent fault (error counter overflow), the normal central processing subsystem is reconfigured by the rotation method, utilizing the emergency action control circuit. Also, the input-output and speech path subsystems are reconfigured, by their own rotation method, thus re-establishing a call processing system. When the system is reconfigured by initiating the emergency action control circuit, the speech path terminal units are initialised to set up the conditions required for resuming the switching operation. Then call processing is resumed at a fixed point.

8.4 Application of reconfiguration

8.4.1 Central processing subsystem

When a fault is detected in the central processing system, normal service is restored by reconfiguring the subsystem. The fault is detected by a trigger from the emergency action circuit (EMG). The principle of the technique used may be understood by a simple example shown in Fig. 8.4. In this example there are two central controls (CC0 and CC1) and two temporary memory modules (TM0 and TM1). There are therefore four ways of configuring a working central processing subsystem.

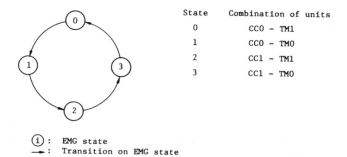

State	Combination of units
0	CC0 – TM1
1	CC0 – TM0
2	CC1 – TM1
3	CC1 – TM0

(i) : EMG state
→ : Transition on EMG state

Fig. 8.4 *Emergency (EMG) state rotation control*

When the EMG circuit is triggered due to a fault in the subsystem the reconfiguration technique is to simply rotate the configuration and attempt to restart call processing. Assuming only a single fault has occurred, a working configuration will be re-established by 1 or 2 reconfigurations.

In practice there will be several TMs as these are provided on an N working module plus 1 spare (i.e. $N+1$ modules rather than full duplication, or $2N$ modules). If, for example, there are five working modules required to operate the system and six are provided, there are 12 possible working configurations as shown in Fig. 8.5. At any one

Pattern number (Note)	5	4	3	2	1	THU	CCI	CCO
0	o	o	o	o		o		o
1	o	o	o	o	o			o
2	o	o	o	o		o	o	
3 (Example)	o	o	o	o	o		o	
4	o	o		o	o	o		o
5	o	o	o		o	o		o
6	o	o		o	o	o	o	
7	o	o	o		o	o	o	
8		o	o	o	o	o		o
9	o		o	o	o	o		o
10		o	o	o	o	o	o	
11	o		o	o	o	o	o	

o ⵗ Connected

(Note)　For pattern number, a valid pattern is selected from the memory installation table. An invalid pattern is skipped.

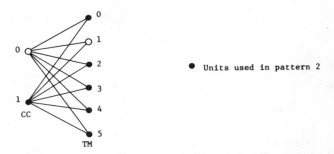

● Units used in pattern 2

Fig. 8.5　*Central processing subsystem reconfiguration pattern*

time the system will be in one of these configurations and when a fault is detected the configuration is changed to the next pattern in the list. Assuming only a single fault, eventually a working system will be re-established. In practice, it has been found that an average of 2·3 reconfigurations are required to re-establish a working system. Note that the current pattern number is recorded on the magnetic drum, so as to be used as a next rotation starting pattern.

8.4.2 Speech path subsystem

This Section describes reconfiguration of the switch controller (SC) as an example, since the same reconfiguration method is applicable for all the equipment in the speech path subsystem. It is also applicable to equipment of the input-output subsystems. Fig. 8.6 shows an example of the reconfiguration pattern used for a signal receiver-distributor (SRD) and an SC. The load on the failed SC is switched over to the standby SC. Since the drive order to the SC is issued by the CC through the SRD, either of these units (CC, SRD and SC) may have a class A fault in many cases.

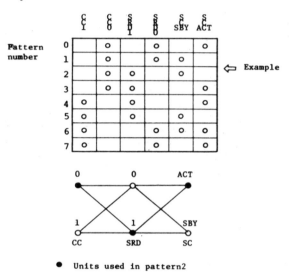

Fig. 8.6   *SC system reconfiguration pattern*

8.5 Restart processing

The cutover of a telephone exchange requires loading of programs, data initialisation and the initialisation of all units. If a fault occurs or equipment configuration changes during the switching operation after the cutover there will be a discontinuous change in the switching system status. To continue to process calls normally it is necessary to perform some resetting so that the system can follow the change. This action is called a restart processing. There are four levels available, depending on the degree of initialisation required (in other words, upon the severity of the reconfiguration). The four levels are called: phase 0, phase 0·5, phase 1 and phase 2.

Triggering of the EMG circuit or the occurrence of a program error may destroy all the data in a temporary memory (TM) that has been used for call processing. When the system is restarted in such a situation, it will not operate properly and, moreover, there may be the risk of propagating the adverse effect of the fault. Accordingly, these pieces of data must be reset to specified initial values. In this case, the simplest way is to set all the data to the initial state. However, established calls will then have to be cleared and this will seriously degrade the service as seen by the users. For this reason, calls in most stable states or in a talking state are retained.

The process through which the calls in talking state are retained is referred to as *phase 0·5 restart processing* when the data stored in the TM is utilised. If this method fails, another restart process will be executed, using data which has been saved on the magnetic drum every five seconds. This is referred to as *phase 1 restart processing.*

Phase 0 restart processing is performed after an error has been processed due to class A interrupt or after equipment configuration has been changed. Since this processing does not interfere with call processing, only simple internal conditions are reinitialised. *Phase 2 restart processing* initialises the switching system at the cutover of the telephone exchange or when it recovers from system breakdown and this involves forcibly clearing all established calls.

Thus, the restart processes are designed to move in the order of phase 0, phase 0·5, phase 1 and phase 2 according to the degree of severity of the fault. The structure of these restart processings is shown in Fig. 8.7 and comparison of the functions is listed in Table 8.2

In the periodic maintenance test of the EMG circuit, the system is restored by a phase 0·5 restart processing, since the EMG circuit is not actually initiated by a fault (data on TN secured).

8.5.1 Details of phase restart processes

Phase 0 (Fig. 8.8): Although call processing is interrupted for a moment, due to occurrence of a fault, it is returned to the interrupted point, since it is not affected due to an error or after equipment reconfiguration.

Phase 0·5: These restart processes are used to restore the switching system in those instances where a fault causing the initiation of the EMG circuit or program confusion has occurred during the switching operation. The data in the TM required for call processing may be destroyed. To maintain the continutiy of service as far as possible, only the calls in talking state are kept that are in a relatively stable state

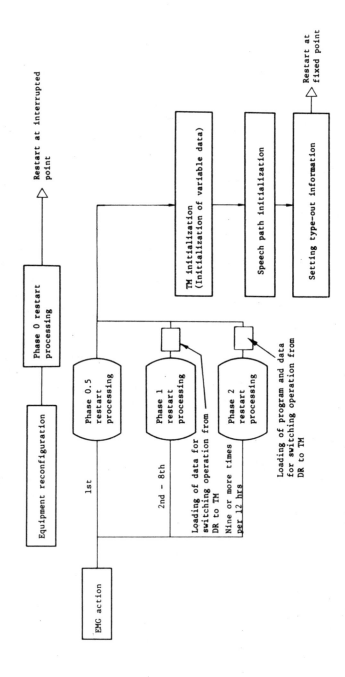

Fig. 8.7 *Restart processing structure*

Table 8.2 *Restart process comparison*

Item	Phase 0	Phase 0·5	Phase 1	Phase 2
Initiating factor	· Equipment fault · Equipment configuration change	· EMG circuit initiated once per 12 hr	· EMG circuit initiated two to eight times per 12 hr	· EMG circuit initiated nine times or more per 12 hr
Call relief	All	Calls in talking state (with data on temporary memory)	Calls in talking state (with data on magnetic drum)	None
Call processing interrupted period	Several hundred ms	8 – 12 s	20 – 50 s	Approximately 3 min
Initialisation	——	· Equipment used by initialised calls in speech path subsystem · Data on temporary memory (except calls in talking state)	· All equipment in the speech path subsystem except those used by calls in talking state · Data on temporary memory (except calls in talking state)	· All equipment · Data on temporary memory

during the restart processing time (approximately 10 to 30 s). All calls during state transition are initialised. In this way, call processing is restarted. The method of maintaining established calls uses the call processing progress state which is mainly stored in the trunk memory (TM). The consistency of this data is checked by utilising the inherent redundancy. Calls which pass these tests are retained.

This method is a phase 0·5 restart. When this restart proves ineffective, a phase 1 restart is initiated.

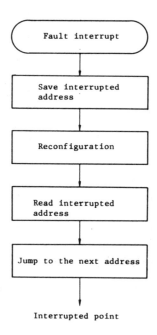

Fig. 8.8 *Phase 0 restart processing*

Phase 1: During normal operation the data in the trunk memories is copied onto the magnetic drum every five seconds. In a phase 1 restart the latest copy of this data is read back into the trunk memories so as to attempt to keep the calls in talking state.

Generally, in the normal operation of the switching system, all the hardware states are stored by software, and a complete match is assured between both states. Accordingly, both hardware and software are set to the initial values when the system is restarted at an uncertain state. For a phase 1 restart, however, attempts are made to continue the calls which were in the talking state on the occurrence of a fault without initialisation. The data used at the time are call data saved 5 to 10 s before. It should be noted that there is not always a match between the present states of hardware and the call data, due to possible presence of calls already cleared and disconnected at the restart, calls waiting for disconnect processing at the clearing (including calls disconnected during the restart process itself) or calls placed in talking state from ringing. For this reason, it is necessary to confirm, through trunk scanning, that those calls for which there are stored data indicated as being the talking state, are in fact still off-hook. These tests are summarised by Fig. 8.9

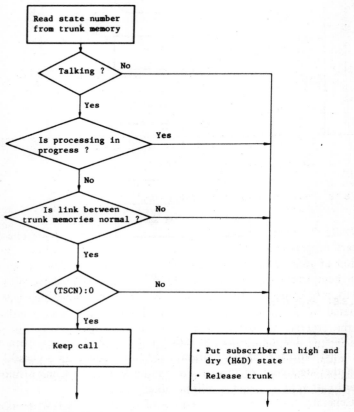

Fig. 8.9   *Calls relief logic*

Fig. 8.10 shows correlation between various states of calls and the effect of this call retention process.

In this way, the phase 0·5 or 1 restart processing program initialises both hardware and software, thus allowing the system to self-recover from a serious fault.

At the time of system restart some temporary trafffic congestion may take place, caused by calls waiting for disconnection and off-hook detection. Arrangements are made in call processing so as to prevent such irregular traffic loads from occurring at the restart time.

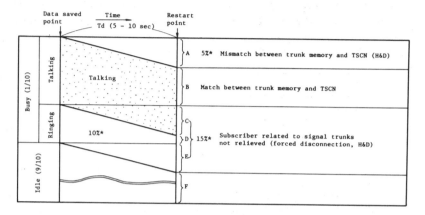

```
*:  Rate to busy subscribers when Td=7.5 sec.
B:  Relieved
A, C, D, E:  Initialized
```

Fig. 8.10 *Subscriber state and relief processing*

Phase 2: When the switching operation is restored by a phase 1 restart process, the EMG circuit may be retriggered within a short period of time. This means that the system cannot recover from the fault completely with a phase 1 restart, resulting in repeated phase 1 restart processings. In such a case, phase 2 restart processing will be initiated by the maintenance engineer's intervention or automatically by the program to perform more complete initialisation. In this processing, the commonly used equipment is completely reconfigured at the initial stage. Speech path terminal equipment is also completely initialised. Since all the calls are initialised, the call processing will be interrupted for approximately three minutes.

8.6 Reconfiguration unit status

When a fault is encountered in a unit, the load will be switched over to a standby unit, the faulty unit being isolated. In a periodic test, the maintenance engineer will isolate equipment or change the active system. Also, equipment extensions will be made from time to time. Such changes in the equipment state are administered by the program and are processed without leading to disorder by various requests.

The state of common equipment is classified as follows:

> installed
> under construction
> out of service
> standby
> unusable owing to a fault of the higher ranking equipment in the input output subsystem.

Definitions of equipment states are shown in Table 8.3.

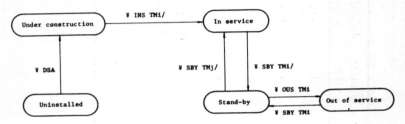

Fig. 8.11   *Equipment states transition*

The maintenance engineer can change the operating state of the equipment by typing in a command, as shown.

(1) ¥OUS:* Isolates a unit from the active systems and blocks it (*out of service*)

(2) ¥INS: Incorporates the isolated unit into the active system (*in service*)

(3) ¥SBY: Switches the designated unit over to standby to place it in a standby state

(4) ¥DSA: Updates the installation table to place the unit in an installed state.

These commands are executed under specified conditions, since a switching system is affected considerably by these command executions. Unless the conditions are satisfied, the command is not executed. Fig. 8.11 illustrates the transition of the memory states, together with the command operations.

---

* Editor's note: ¥ is the Yen sign corresponding to £ or $ on a western typewriter.

Table 8.3   *Equipment states definitions*

Equipment State	Installation table	Construction table	Trouble table	Standby table	Unusable table	Remarks
Uninstalled	0	0	0	0	(1)	Not installed
Under construction	1	1	0	0	(1)	Similar to out of service
In service	1	0	0	0	(0)	Usable
Out of service	1	0	1	0	(1)	Recognised fault by an operator
Standby	1	0	0	1	(1)	Temporary fault or being used in a standby system
Unusable	1	0	0	0	1	Higher ranking equipment is not usable in the input output system

8.7 Fault message type-out

An occurrence of a trouble, such as a fault or an error in common equipment, a program error or a trouble with the master timer, will alert a maintenance engineer by means of message output, alarms or lamp display. The message output and lamp display are activated by the fault report processing program, while alarms are given individually in the course of restart processing and fault processing. It is necessary, however, to comprehensively administer the alarms in the system, so that control is made by the alarm programs on a macro or subroutine basis. The alarm program is called when required in the restart processing. Described below are fault report processing classified by information content.

Message output: The fault report processing program is initiated, upon an occurrence of a fault, to type out the fault information; it is not required to run the program under normal circumstances. If the program were initiated directly by the fault processing program, however, the processing would be performed at the same program execution level as the fault processing execution level. The fault report processing should be performed at the base level after call processing has been resumed. To do this, the following method is used.

Data, such as fault type and fault state, from each fault processing program, are stored in a data transfer area called a *fault processing hopper*. This primes the fault report processing program. The fault report processing program at the base level unloads the data from the fault processing hopper and clears the hopper. Based upon the stored data, the program formats the type-out message and calls for the type-out processing.

Also, it stores the equivalent of the type-out information in the magnetic drum to collect the fault statistics data.

Out of service (OS) lamp: For a fault or equipment isolation a lamp OS flashes on the supervisory and test frame and the corresponding equipment frame. It is controlled by a lamp OS program which contains one bit of memory assigned to each lamp OS, and the control table is provided to check the state of lamp OS.

Alarm: Subroutines are provided to activate major and minor alarms indicated by lamps and bells. Upon activation of the restart processing, the required subroutine is called to provide alarm control. A control table is also provided similarly to lamp OS. When each subroutine is executed, the signal distributor is controlled on the basis of the table.

The alarm control table is used for alarm control over the entire system. For example, even if an alarm off is requested by the program, due to recovery of a fault, the request will be ignored when another equipment fault is found in the control table.

Chapter 9

Maintenance and administration programs

So far the functions of the switching system itself have been described. There are, however, various administrative tasks that require human intervention to maintain the switching system in a good serviceable condition.

The administrative tasks for the continuous maintenance of switching service are various and diverse. They include:

(a) testing the subscriber lines and speech paths
(b) preventive maintenance testing
(c) diagnosis of common equipment faults
(d) monitoring and recording traffic conditions for statistical data
(e) inspecting service quality
(f) updating subscriber data each time they change
(g) accounting
(h) equipment extension.

Since these functions can be performed by co-operation of maintenance engineer and programs, a means of communication is required between the engineer and the switching system.

9.1 The man-machine interface*

Conventional systems such as a crossbar are provided with lamps, keys, punched cards etc., as a means of communication between the engineer and the machine. This is commonly known as *man-machine communication*.

---

* Editor's note: This is the form used in the original D-10 system. Since its introduction, the CCITT have standardised on a universal man-machine language which would be used on any new ESS.

In an electronic switching system, however, the system and the operator exchange information solely through a teletypewriter unit.

To input a command, the engineer depresses the request key on the teletypewriter and when the system is ready to accept the command it prints ¥ℏℏ (where ℏ indicates the blank character). A command is then entered with the general format

Component	Construction
function code	a three-letter combination indicating required program
parameter 1 parameter N	detail required, up to 5 parameters preceded by blanks
end of command	final parameter followed by slant sign /

The commands relating to data modifications are normally prepared on paper tape and entered via the teletypewriter reader. These tapes are kept as a record of commands entered and could be used in the event of a complete program restart. When a large volume of data is entered, such as required during an extension, the parameters only may be entered on paper tape. In this case the format of the parameter is as follows:

$$Pi, Pi + 1, Pi + 2, \ldots, Pi + n/ \ldots / \text{PEND} /$$

The symbol ',' separates each parameter, '/' is for the termination of a group of parameters, and 'PEND' indicates the end of all parameters.

Parameter entry format

The meaning of the parameter fields varies with the command used. The parameters can refer to a wide variety of items such as terminal equipment, directory numbers, digits, etc. They are expressed in a format specific to the switching system and therefore to avoid confusion the entry format must be chosen so as to coincide with the form which is frequently used in maintenance work or with the designations of equipment units and frames. At the same time, it should coincide with that form of any output message from the system.

The format which is used for input and output from the system is called the '*physical name expression*', as distinct from the '*logical name expression*' which is used by programs within the switching system.

Table 9.1 gives some examples of the form of physical name expressions for common units, such as central control, memory and

Table 9.1 Parameter entry format

Classification	General format	Code	Meaning
Common unit	ABCxxyy	ABC	Types of units. Expressed by 1 to 4 alphabetic letters
		xx	Subsystem number (Decimal notation). The number length depends on the number of subsystem
		yy	Unit number. The number length depends on the number of units
Terminal number	A : xx x	A	Terminal number class. Expressed by one alphabetic letter
		:	Separator between terminal class and its number
		xx x	Terminal number
	Letters	Three alphabetic letters	e.g. REG (registration), OUT (output)
Others	Characters	Eight alphabetic letters or less	Special symbols b, ' , ; , / , : , @ and ¥ cannot be used
	Slip format	—	Slip format is input from paper tape when subscriber translator is updated

Table 9.2 *Parameter expression example*

Meaning	Example
Temporary memory #2 (unit number)	TM2
Signal receiver-distributor 0 in SPCE#1 (subsystem number)	SRD10
Standby switch controller (of SPCE#1)	STSC1
Line link network switch controller 2 in SPCE#0 (subsystem number)	LSCO2
Teletypewriter unit in CH#1 and TPC#0 (subsystem number)	TYP10
Trunk number	$\text{T:}\ \underset{\text{TB}}{\underline{XX}}\ \underset{\text{TSG}}{\underline{XX}}\ \underset{\text{TU}}{\underline{XX}}$
Line equipment number	$\text{E:}\ \underset{\text{NW}}{\underline{{}^{L}\!/_{T}\,XX}}\ \underset{\text{SG}}{\underline{X}}\ \underset{\text{G}}{\underline{XX}}\ \underset{\text{SW}}{\underline{X}}\ \underset{\text{LV}}{\underline{X}}$ L...LLN T...TLN
Trunk group number	R: XXX

Table 9.2 *contd.,*

Meaning	Example
Link number	L: $^A/_B$ $^L/_T$ XX X XX X X A . . . Link A . . . . B . . . Link B $\underbrace{\quad}_{\text{Link}}$ $\underbrace{\text{NW}\quad\text{SG}}$ $\underbrace{\text{G}\quad\text{SW}\quad\text{LV}}$ XXXX
Path number	P: $^L/_T$ $\underbrace{\text{XXXXX . . . . XXXX}}_{\text{NW}}$
Grid number	G: $^L/_T$ XX $^J/_S$ $\underbrace{\text{XX}}_{\text{G}}$ $\underbrace{\qquad}_{\text{NW}}$
Directory number	N: XX X
PM/TM address	A: HH . . . . H
DR address	D: $\overset{*1}{X}$ $\underbrace{\text{H . . . . H}}_{\text{Address}}$ $\overset{*1}{}$ Drum unit number
Hexadecimal notation	H: HH . . . . H
Decimal notation	XX X
Message	M: ABC . . . . Z

speech path control equipment, and terminal numbers such as trunk, line equipment number and directory number. Table 9.2 gives some specific examples. Means are provided to correct or cancel a command.

9.2 Command analysis

The types of commands are classified as follows according to the functions:

> Command control (e.g. command execution stop and output printing stop)
> System control (e.g. system configuration change, blocking or release of common equipment)
> Test and diagnosis of equipment
> System extension
> Administration (e.g. selection of observation numbers and collection of statistical data)
> Debug

When a command is entered, the physical name expression must be converted into the logical name expression so that it may be used by the program. At the same time the command must be checked to ensure that the input syntax is correct and to determine and activate the program required. These functions are performed by the *command analysis program*.

The commands are executed by the *command execution program*. This program can be stored on the magnetic drum as it does not require as much real-time processing as does the call processing program. Because of this, the command function program is constructed as a series of modules. Individual functions are divided and assigned to modules, so that a command function is processed by the combination of the modules. The module here is called the '*command element*', while a combination of elements is called the '*command unit*'. The execution sequence of command elements and their parameters is specified by the *command unit table*. Commands are executed according to this unit table, by the command execution control.

The command processing flow is shown in Fig. 9.1. Command processing is activated by the teletypewriter unit input which communicates with the teletypewriter control program (execution control program) at the command input stage. After the request key is pressed by the engineer the command acceptance ready sign is output. The input characters are read up to the '/' symbol, and then the execution

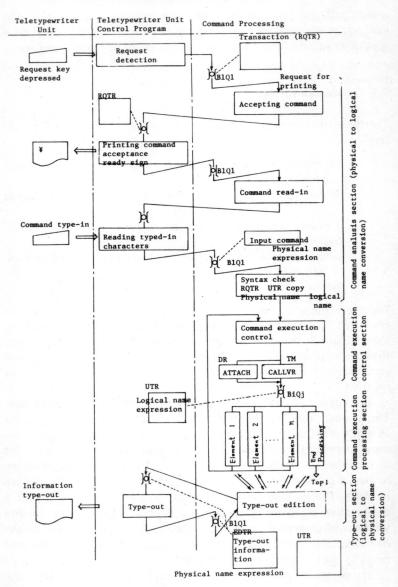

Fig. 9.1   *Command processing flow*

of the command is started. After the syntactical check of the command the program converts the parameter part from physical to logical name and enters the command execution control section. In this Section a series of command elements is executed as specified by the contents of the command unit table for the appropriate command.

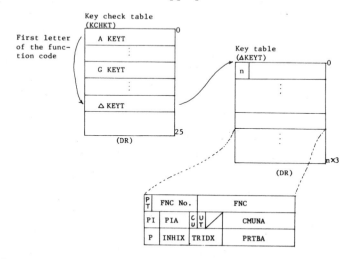

PT: Indication of inputs only from paper tapes
PI: Initial PI value
PIA: Auxiliary PI
CU: Command unit decision indicator
P: 00 Indicates that there is no parameter next.
    01 Indicates that the next parameter can be omitted.
    10 Indicates that the next parameter is loaded from the paper tape.
    11 Indicates that the next parameter cannot be omitted.
INHIX: Inhibit pattern index
TRIDX: UTR size index
        5;   32W
        6;   64
        7; 128
        ⋮
CMUNA: Command unit table address, or auxiliary table address
PRTBA: Parameter table address
UT: Storage class (TM/DR) of command unit table

Fig. 9.2 *Key table structure*

When output messages are required these are edited by the type-out editing program and output by the teletypewriter unit control program.

Some details of the main components of the command processing system are described below.

Request detection: When the teletypewriter unit control program detects a request command, it seizes a request transaction record

(RQTR), and loads it with the command acceptance symbol and adds it to the queue for print-out. The engineer's response to the command acceptance signal is stored in the RQTR which is added to the queue for the function code recognition program.

Function code recognition: The function code is decoded by the command analysis program by means of a *key check table* and associated *key tables*, all stored on the magnetic drum. These tables have the structure shown in Fig. 9.2. The key check table is indexed by the first character of the function code which if it is valid points to a key table. The key table is searched looking for a match on the remaining two characters.

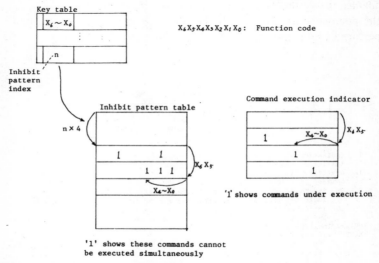

Fig. 9.3   *Method of checking command interference*

The format of the key table entries is also shown in Fig. 9.2. One of the entries specifies the required size of a universal transaction record (UTR) required for the particular command. The command analysis program seizes a suitable UTR and copies the input data from the RQTR to the UTR. The RQTR is then released. This is because the size of transaction required depends on the command and the RQTR is expected to be released as soon as possible to accept the next type-in. After the RQTR is released, another command input is possible from the same teletypewriter unit.

To prevent commands from interfering with each other, the program checks whether commands which can cause mutual interference are being executed. This check is performed with the use of the command execution table and the *inhibit pattern table*, as shown in Fig. 9.3. The inhibit pattern table is prepared for each group of commands which may interfere with each other. The appropriate inhibit pattern table is referenced in the key table. If it is found that no interfering commands are being executed, an execution indicator is set and the control proceeds to the next processing stage.

The program next checks the command attribute. The D-10 electronic switching system provides a guard against commands such as ¥MLD (manual load) and ¥FST (forcible set) which can adversely affect the system if inadvertently typed-in. Guarded and nonguarded states are established by the program for each teletypewriter unit. This enables the system to reject these commands if they are typed-in under the guarded state. Turning the guarded state into a nonguarded one is performed by command ¥GDR (guard release).

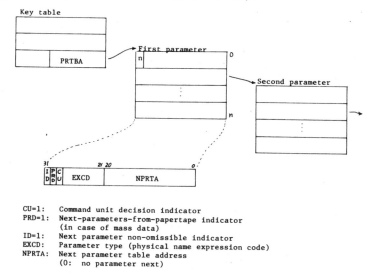

```
CU=1:   Command unit decision indicator
PRD=1:  Next-parameters-from-papertape indicator
        (in case of mass data)
ID=1:   Next parameter non-omissible indicator
EXCD:   Parameter type (physical name expression code)
NPRTA:  Next parameter table address
        (0:  no parameter next)
```

Fig. 9.4   *Parameter table structure*

Parameter check and conversion into logical name expression
Syntactical correctness of the command parameters is checked with the parameter table. The parameter table (shown in Fig. 9.4) is stored on the magnetic drum and linked with the key table. If several types of parameters are permitted in a position, then as many parameter tables are prepared. Parameters are checked by a key search method, where each parameter is taken as the key.

Maintenance and administration programs

Page 164

Table 9.3 Physical and logical name expression example

Parameter	Physical name expression	Logical name expression	Remarks
Central control	CC0	`3 1` / `0 0`	Logical name of common equipment is reconfiguration number
Switch controller (for LLN)	LSC02 (SPC)	`5 6` / `16 4`	
Channel multiplexer	CHM0	`4 13` / `2 0`	
Line link network	LLN12 (SPC)	*1 `5 75` / `0 1 2`	*1: 1 for TLN

Table 9.3   *contd.,*

Parameter	Physical name expression	Logical name expression	Remarks
Trunk number	T: 13 06 03 TB TSG TU	13 6 3 6 64	
Line equipment number	E: L03 2 18 7 0 NW SG G SW LV	*1 00 3 2 18 7 0 8 65	
Directory number	N: 2676009	0 9 10 10 6 7 6 2 7 70 0 0 0	
Hexadecimal number	H: 2A0B	0 0 0 2 10 0 11 4 73	

Crossed fields are all zeros

The parameters, which are input syntactically correct, are converted into a logical name expression. The result of the conversion by the command analysis is represented by two words, as shown in Table 9.3. The function code of the command is also converted into a logical name expression.

Thus, the function code and the parameters are checked before execution of the command begins. If the check result is NO GOOD, the check number (event no.) associated with each check point is passed to a type-out editor program to be typed-out as an error number. Maintenance engineers can interpret the error by referring to an error interpretation manual.

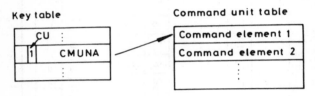

(1) Decided by Function Code

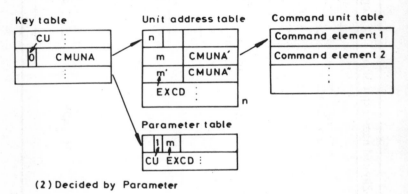

(2) Decided by Parameter

Fig. 9.5   *Command unit table decision*
CU Command unit decision indicator
CMUNA Command unit table address or auxiliary table address
EXCD Parameter type (physical name expression code)

Command unit table selection

The command functions required are specified in a command unit table. The required table is selected by a key search method using as a key the function code and/or the parameter code. The method of selection is shown in Fig. 9.5.

When the command unit table is to be determined by the function code, the CU indicator in the key table is '1' and the command unit table address is in the CMUNA field. When it is to be determined by the parameters, the CMUNA field specifies an auxiliary address table. This address table contains the physical name expression codes of parameters as key holes and the unit table addresses to be used when a match occurs. The parameter list (Fig. 9.4) contains its own CU indicator. At some stage of the parameters being matched against the parameter list, the CU indicator will be 1 and at that stage the auxiliary unit address table will be accessed to obtain the command unit table address. Thus, the command unit table is chosen in the process of checking the function code or checking the parameters.

9.3 Command execution

In the ESS command system, a command processing program is not provided for each command function. Instead, individual commands are processed by a program consisting of a combination of necessary basic functions as specified in the command unit table. This approach decreases the memory required for programs, reduces the overlay area occupancy time, provides an easy division of overlay programs, and simplifies the arrangement of command processing units. Sequential execution of these command elements is controlled by the command execution control program (Fig. 9.6). This program has three main functions:

(i) *Reading the command element:* The command element to be executed next is read from the chosen command unit table at an address specified by a step-counter (STPC). When the command element is present in the main memory (TM), the program starting address and required priority level is read. The program starting address is copied into the UTR which is then attached to the base level queue of the appropriate priority. When the command element is on the magnetic drum, the table is read into the overlay program area and activated after it has been read into main memory.

(ii) *Program activation:* The format of the command element is shown in Fig. 9.7. The function part specifies a program associated with that element. Most programs are stored on the magnetic drum and they must first be read into main memory before they can be executed.

(iii) *Updating of step-counter (STPC):* If the command element indicates that it is the last element, control is returned to the base level controller, otherwise control is returned to the command control program after the execution of each command element. Normally the step-counter is incremented so as to extract the command element

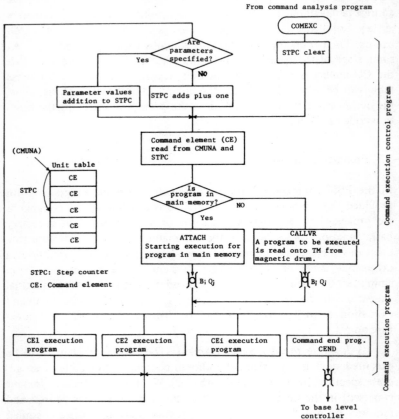

Fig. 9.6 *Command execution control*

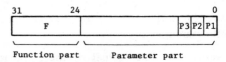

Fig. 9.7 *Command element composition*

from the table. However, it is possible to provide branching and looping by means of special command units which return a parameter to the command control. Table 9.4 lists the common command elements and Fig. 9.8 illustrates how they effect the repetition flow.

Table 9.4   *Common element for command execution control*

Code	Description
JPF	Jump forward
JPB	Jump backward
RPT	Command element repetition
PRD	Paper tape read
CEND	Command end processing

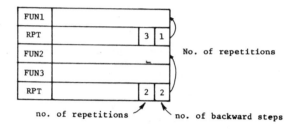

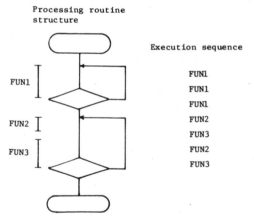

Fig. 9.8   *Repetition flow example*

9.4 Output message editing

Messages that are output from an ESS are of two categories; one is output in response to an engineer's input during traffic observation and test or diagnosis of faults, and the other is output autonomously to notify the user of a 'no good' result of a continuity test or fault of common equipment during call processing and traffic congestion. Each message output is produced by requests generated by ESS programs. In general, all data exchange between the CC and IO is controlled by a service program called IOCS.

The message editor program is part of IOCS and this program requires as input the information to be output plus an indication of the required output format.

The message format is simplified through combinations of basic formats of various messages which cover all the message formats. This provides a standardisation for each maintenance program and also simplifies the message editor program. Table 9.5 illustrates the basic formats and with some examples of printing.

Table 9.5   *Basic message printing format example*

Control code	Significance		Printing format example
B	Data specified in 〈 of binary number	〉 are output in the form	101110
D	Data specified in 〈 of decimal number	〉 are output in the form	2130
H	Data specified in 〈 of hexadecimal number	〉 are output in the form	00AD90
T	Data specified in 〈 of trunk number	〉 are output in the form	T: 100112
N	Data specified in 〈 of directory number	〉 are output in the form	N: 5093126
U	Data specified in 〈 of common equipment number	〉 are output in the form	DRU00 TSC01

Each maintenance program generates the necessary messages using the control codes of printing basic formats shown in Table 9.5. A table which specifies output formats by a control code of a single alphabetic character and data (or data address) is referred to as *format table*. Fig. 9.9 shows an example of a format table and Fig. 9.10 illustrates a printing example produced from that table.

The message editor program takes the output information and the format designator and writes the required output message (in ISO code) into an edit transaction memory record (EDTR). The editor program then requests the teletypewriter unit control program to print necessary message line by line. After completion of editing and printing, control is returned to the program which had requested the message output.

The message editor program repeats editing and printing for individual lines. It checks the queue for a request of higher priority after printing of each line. If there is a higher priority request waiting, the processing under way is suspended to make way for the processing of the higher priority.

```
X8F<# EXAMPLE #>X3Y//F<EX1>X2P
<0>X2F<EX2>(4,1-X1D1<1:10,4>)1
F<EX3>X2N7<6>F<-XYZ>//X8F<# EN
D #>%
```

Fig. 9.9   *Format table example*

```
# EXAMPLE #    12/31 24:00    (A)

EX1 P:L0232062-2-106    EX2  0 2 4 8
EX3 N:5094131-XYZ
        # END #
```

Fig. 9.10   *Printing example*

The processing under way is continued when the queue contains only the requests for processing with the same or lower priority order.

The following are the three priority orders for message output:

   (i) Highest priority – request acceptance, conversational type response, etc.

 (ii) Higher priority – fault messages

(iii) Normal priority – other messages

9.5 Testing of subscriber lines, trunks and the network

This Section describes the tests of equipment or components which constitute a speech path; a test for localising a faulty point when a fault occurs or a test conducted as preventive maintenance.

9.5.1 Subscriber line tests

The electronic switching system is provided with various convenient features to test the subscriber lines in addition to conventional exchange features.

   (i) *Test at line test frame:* A command is provided which causes the connection of a test circuit in the line test frame to the subscriber line. This allows a test engineer to test its capacity, insulation resistance, dial characteristics and so on.

(ii) *Route trace:* The route (path and trunk) through which a particular subscriber is connected can be traced by utilising the connection path information. This makes it convenient to troubleshoot a subscriber line. When the directory number of a particular subscriber is specified by a command (¥RTR for example) this number is translated into the line equipment number (LEN). The trunk memories are searched looking for this LEN. Once found the trunk memories contain the path memory, trunk number and call state — all of which are typed-out.

(iii) *Automatic line test:* This test is used for preventive maintenance or an installation test. When the ¥ALT command is typed in, the designated subscriber lines are automatically connected one by one to automatic line test equipment (ALTE). The command is of the form

$$\text{¥ALT N: XX} \ldots \text{X,} \quad \begin{array}{c} \text{number of} \\ \text{subscriber lines} \\ \text{to be tested} \end{array} \quad \text{(time designation)/}$$

where XX . . . X is the directory number with which the test is to be started. The automatic line test equipment performs insulation resistance and capacity tests between A/B wires and ground and between A and B wires and evaluates the results, which will be typed out.

It is possible to specify the time at which this test is to be started. Omission of time causes an immediate start of the test. If the time is set so as to start the test at a nonbusy hour, e.g. at night, it will be possible to analyse the results the next day.

When it is started by a program with a subscriber line connected to ALTE, as shown in Fig. 9.11, ALTE automatically performs the insulation resistance test and the capacity test and outputs the results to the scanner. The program reads the scanner periodically, evaluates the test result information of the scanner and outputs the results.

9.5.2 Trunk circuit test

A trunk test is performed by means of the speech path test equipment (SPTE), and a trunk connection to SPTE is administered by a program. The trunk to be tested is not connected by an exclusive program, but is processed normally except that its origination type indicates that it is a test. For example, with a test call originated from an originating test line (OTL) terminal, normal processing applies, except that the previously designated trunk is selected and connected (called a preset connection). The function of the trunk test programs therefore is to mark a trunk group to be in the preset condition, block the trunk to be tested, or to change the class of the originating/terminating terminal according to the specified trunk.

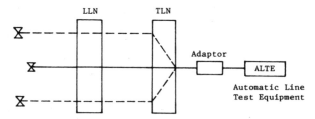

Fig. 9.11   *Subscriber line connection*

There are two methods of testing a trunk; manual connection test and automatic connection test.

9.5.2.1 Manual connection test: This test may be used as a speech path test made for each service call, a confirmation test to analyse a trouble found in an automatic connection test (described later), and as a functional check of a trunk before it is put into service when the system is being expanded.

The test causes a test call generated by the speech path test equipment (SPTE) to seize the trunk circuit under test, and uses the circuit in the process of establishing the call to confirm its function. This feature permits the testing of all trunk circuits appearing on the switch network. Fig. 9.12 illustrates the connection patterns for the originating and terminating trunks as typical examples.

The originating trunk is tested in the process of terminating the call from the originating test line terminal (OTL) of SPTE to the automatic answer trunk (AAT) or automatic connection test trunk (ACTT) in an associated exchange. The test process starts with the maintenance engineer typing-in the command ¥MCT to specify the class of OTL and the trunk to be tested (test preparation). Then, the engineer operates the keys and dial on the SPTE to repeatedly generate test calls, and confirms the results by ear or lamp display. When the RLS key is thrown, the test will be complete.

The terminating trunk is tested in such a way that an incoming trunk (ICT) is seized from incoming line test frame (ICLTF) and the call is terminated by the terminating test line (TTL) terminal through the ICT under test. In this case, the call is orginated from OTL and is connected to required ICT through the test outgoing trunk (OGT), SPTE and ICLTF. The operations at the distant exchange are simulated by utilising the call processing program of the same exchange. Thus an ordinary OGT can be used for the test OGT. This test is performed by first

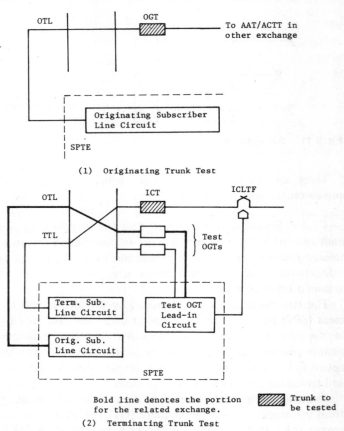

(1) Originating Trunk Test

(2) Terminating Trunk Test

Bold line denotes the portion for the related exchange.

Trunk to be tested

Fig. 9.12   *Connection pattern in manual connection test*
ICLTF Incoming line test frame

physically connecting the ICT to the SPTE at the ICLTF and then typing in the command ¥MCT to designate the test ICT. The test program will now cause the connection of the test OGT to the SPTE, with the appropriate signalling system of the designated ICT. The program will also designate the use of the test OGT in call processing, and give the ICT a test call indication. When the test engineer throws the make busy (MB) key on the SPTE, the test OGT and the ICT will be commanded to send a blocking signal to OGT in the distant exchange. The subsequent test operations are now the same as for an originating trunk.

The process of seizing the designated trunk is as follows. First, the program blocks the trunk specified by the parameter of command ¥MCT. It also sets an indicator that the particular trunk group number contains a blocked trunk. If the trunk is busy, the program applies prior blocking to it, waiting for the existing call to complete before it blocks the trunk. When the blocking is complete, a lamp lights to inform the test engineer that all is ready. If now a call is identified to be a test call in a subsequent connecting process, the program checks whether the trunk group number requested by the originating call matches the marked trunk group. If there is no match, however, it assumes that the trunk group is not designated, and performs a normal call set-up.

9.5.2.2 *Automatic connection test:* The purpose of this test is for preventive maintenance, and the testing procedures such as a connection method are similar to those for the manual connection test. A program is substituted for manual operations to automate the test. This enables trunk circuits and junction lines to be tested at one time. However, the terminating trunks are excluded from this test, since it is difficult to automatically test the incoming trunk circuit by the program. The program can substitute for the test engineer by enabling a relay controller (RC) or signal distributor (SD) to control the keys and dials on speech path test equipment (SPTE) and by permitting the reading of a lamp display or checking of a tone through a trunk scanner (TSCN). If any of the test items is found unsatisfactory, the trunk number and other test data will be typed out.

This test is performed by typing in command ¥ACT. Viewed from the character of the automatic test, there is a large amount of data for trunk specification and dialling number, so that paper tape is used to read-in the test data. The test is initiated by key STT (start) operation or by a time designating command. A combination of a dial number and a trunk number forms a unit of data on the paper tape, and any number of units can be designated. Also, it is possible to designate trunks in the unit of a trunk group number (TGN). It is assumed that, for an OGT, the call (dialled digits) is terminated at ACTT in the related exchange and, for other trunks, at TTL. Only free trunks are test objects. Busy trunks are skipped in the test.

In a tandem switch (TS), this automatic test includes an automatic trunk line test, which uses automatic trunk testing and transmission measuring equipment to test the trunk lines for working, transmission loss measurement and noise measurement.

9.5.3 Network test

In those instances where a continuity failure or a false connection and ground (FCG) is found in a service call test, the program initiates the fault report processing, causing the teletypewriter unit to report the information on the failed path to the maintenance engineer. A continuity test is made to reproduce and confirm the fault found in call processing. When the maintenance engineer types in the path data reported in call processing, the program reproduces the fault or separates the faulty part in the unit of a network using speech path test equipment (SPTE) or loop continuity test trunk (LPCTT). This enables the maintenance engineer to locate the failed path in the unit of a faulty link by manual operation.

(a) *Speech path continuity test:* The principles of this test are shown in Fig. 9.13. The program sets up a double-connection to the failed path from a special line called the *continuity test line* (CTL). This line connects a resistor to the link and permits the localisation of the failed path to the line or trunk side. The results are typed out and, at the same time, a tracer tone is sent via the CTL so as to enable the maintenance engineer to make a further detailed search for the failed path.

When the maintenance engineer types in the failed path data (¥CNT, originating path data, terminating path data), the test program isolates the failed path and the subscriber/trunk connected to the path from call processing (test preparation). When the start (STT) key is operated, the program establishes the failed path and the path from CTL and, at the same time, makes a localisation of the failed network. The results will be typed out. Operation of the STT key enables the program to repeat the above-mentioned operations. When the RLS key is operated, the test will be completed.

(b) *False connection and ground test (FCG test):* When a trouble is found in the FCG test (which is performed in the normal process of call processing), the FCG test program is initiated automatically. This program controls a double connection of the FCG test circuit to the failed path and opens the crosspoints of the failed path one by one to locate the faulty crosspoint. The results are typed out.

Network link and trunk make-busy and -idle

The command input (¥MKB) permits blocking links or trunks for the speech path test or for package replacement. The unit of blocking is one trunk (trunk make-busy); one link or one grid (link make-busy). The unit is designated in a parameter of the command.

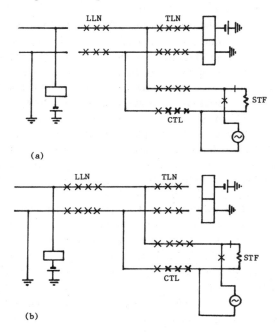

Fig. 9.13   *Test method for continuity tests*
   a TLN — side test
   b LLN — side test
   x normally open contact
   — — normally closed contact

The program is provided with the function for prior-blocking when the designated trunk or link is busy. An MB indication on a trunk memory is used for prior blocking of a trunk. If '1' is written into the trunk memory, the call processing program references it in releasing the trunk, performs the blocking and types out the effect.

The link is not provided with a prior blocking indication. The make-busy program supervises the state of the link every second and carries out the blocking upon detection of a free state.

Command ¥MKI is used to make the blocked trunk or link idle.

9.6 Diagnosis

An occurrence of a trouble in the switching system initiates a hardware interrupt which leads to the execution of a fault processing program. The program identifies the faulty equipment to switch the traffic load over to standby equipment. This reconfigures the system to make it capable of switching operation to restart call processing, thus enabling the system to continue normal switching operation (as described in Chapter 8). Should another item of equipment of the same kind fail during the repair time of the failed equipment, processing of the whole switching system may be suspended. To minimise the probability of occurrence of such a situation, it is necessary to minimise the repair time of the failed item.

Diagnosis in an electronic switching system is more complicated than in the conventional electromagnetic switching system owing to the use of high-speed, miniaturised equipment components. Therefore, program controlled diagnosis is provided for the electronic switching system to automate the diagnosis process as far as possible.

The electronic switching system consists of the common control section, composed of high-speed electronic parts, and the speech path section, composed of electromagnetic parts. The former includes the central control, memory and speech path controller. The latter consists of networks and trunks. Location and repair of a fault differ between the two, in that the speech path section employs methods using the supervisory test frame (STF) and the test commands. The common control section is furnished with a diagnostic function through the diagnosis program.

Diagnosis of the failed equipment is carried out by inputting a diagnostic command through the teletypewriter unit, and the diagnostic results produced by the program are output to the teletypewriter unit. The suspected faulty packages can be found by locating the printout in the *diagnostic dictionary*.

In addition to a diagnosis of the faulty equipment, this diagnostic is used for a confirmation test, after repair of the failed equipment, and can also serve for the installation test and expansion installation test.

9.6.1 The diagnostic role

Fig. 9.14 illustrates the series of procedures needed to repair faulty equipment, up to its incorporation into the active subsystem, including the maintenance engineer's operations.

When a fault occurs in an item of equipment, the fault processing program isolates the item from the system and causes the system to

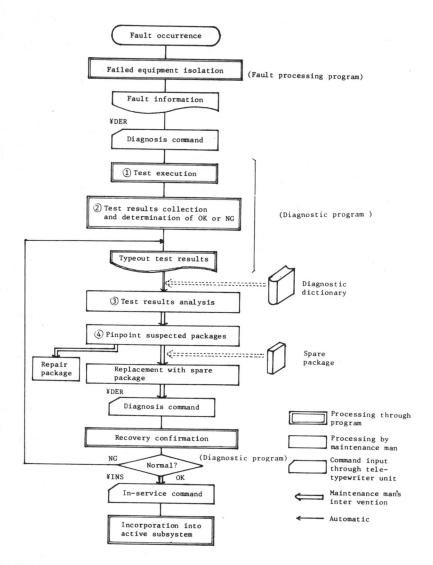

Fig. 9.14 *Fault repair flowchart*

continue the switching operation. The fault information is typed out. The maintenance engineer types in a suitable diagnostic command based on the output information. This diagnostic command signals to the program to start locating the faulty unit. The diagnosis program specified in the command parameters is initiated to execute the test, collect the test results, determine whether they are good or no good, and type out the results. The maintenance engineer, using this information, consults the diagnostic manual and the diagnostic dictionary to determine which of the suspected packages is faulty. The test is rerun by inputting the diagnostic command each time a suspected package is replaced. This action is repeated until good results are obtained, i.e. until the faulty package is replaced. Then, the maintenance engineer types in the in-service command (¥INS) to return the equipment to service. If a faulty package is repaired rather than replaced, it must be given a confirmation test in the same manner as in a fault. The equipment containing the repaired package must first be isolated from the active subsystem (through the out-of-service command (¥OUS)).

The diagnostic command takes the following form:

¥DER P1, P2, P3, P4, P5/

where P1 to P5 are parameters which specify

  P1: the equipment to be diagnosed. Expressed by physical name described in Section 9.2.

  P2: the test phase (range) to be executed. Omission of this parameter means phase 1.

  P3: the diagnostic operation mode which determines the check method of the test result and quantity of information to be typed out. When omitted, the simplest diagnostic operation mode is given.

P4 and P5: further parameters specific to each diagnostic program.

The results of the tests executed are typed out as GOOD or NO GOOD for each test phase. For NO GOOD results detailed information is also printed out. An example of an output when central control 1 is diagnosed is shown in Fig. 9.15. Results of each test phase are output in order.

The output when the result is NO GOOD involves the sample point name, sample clock, result collated with the correct data (all '0's for result 'GOOD') and the correct data as detailed data, which is used for consulting the diagnostic dictionary.

Diagnostic programs

Diagnostic programs are provided for each group of equipment items. A list of the different groups is given in Table 9.6. The individual programs are stored on the drum and are called into main memory overlay area by the *diagnostic supervisory program* which sends the results to the message editor program.

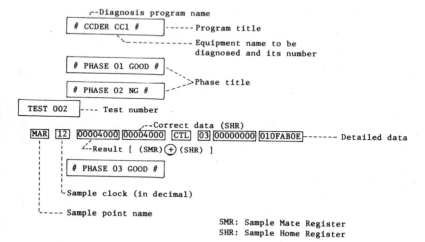

Fig. 9.15 *CC diagnostic program typeout example*

Table 9.6 *Equipment covered by fault diagnosis*

Classification	Equipment name
Central processing subsystem	Central control (CC) Temporary memory (TM) Data channel (CHM and SCH)
Speech path subsystem	Signal receiver and distributor (SRD) Maintenance signal distributor (MSD) Relay controller (RC) Speech path controller (SC) Scanner driver (SCN-DV) Maintenance scanner (MSCN) Scanner (SCN)
Input output subsystem	Magnetic drum equipment (DRC and DR) Magnetic tape equipment (MTC and MTU) Teletypewriter controller (TPC)

Ideally, the diagnostic program should contain sufficient logic to cover every fault. It is, however, impossible to predict and cater for all faults in advance. It is therefore necessary to be able to improve the diagnostic programs as experience is obtained.

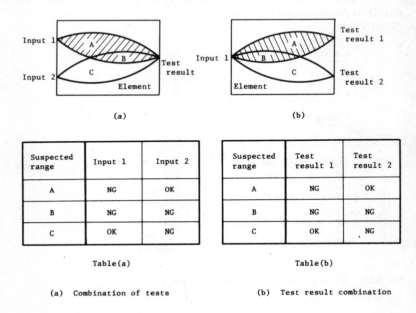

(a)   (b)

Suspected range	Input 1	Input 2
A	NG	OK
B	NG	NG
C	OK	NG

Table(a)

Suspected range	Test result 1	Test result 2
A	NG	OK
B	NG	NG
C	OK	NG

Table(b)

(a)   Combination of tests   (b)   Test result combination

Fig. 9.16   *Suspected range assumption principle*

9.6.2 Diagnostic dictionary

The diagnostic dictionary consists of an output analysis flowchart and a package index table. A dictionary is provided for the diagnostic program associated with each equipment type. The maintenance engineer makes a judgment of the location of a faulty package by checking the output diagnostic results against the diagnostic dictionary. This dictionary takes the form whereby suspected packages are indicated by following the flowchart guided by the test results for each functional unit. The output analysis flowchart is generated by the use of tests which test overlapping parts of the system. Assuming only single faults, the results of a series of tests can be used to locate the suspected area as shown in Fig. 9.16.

Fig. 9.17 shows an example of an output analysis flowchart. Discrimination is made in units test phase between OK and NG, based on the output information. The NG test number group in NG phase is then identified to obtain the index number of the package index table. In the example in Fig. 9.15, index number 02-01 is derived from NG test 2 in NG phase 2. The next step is to consult the package index table shown in Fig. 9.18 for the index number. Column 'SUSPECTED PACK-AGES' presents the package location and its name, and column 'INDEX CONDITION' pinpoints the failed circuitry to a few packages.

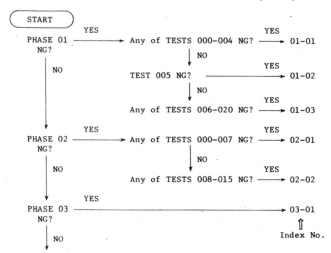

Fig. 9.17 *Output analysis flowchart example*

Index NO.		02-01		INITIAL DIAGNOSIS (Comments on index NO.)	
INDEX CONDITION				SUSPECTED PACKAGES	REMARKS
TEST NO.	SAMPLE POINT CLOCK	RESULT			
TEST 00	CTL6	0000000D		2819 (BL23) 2820 (BL13) 2821 (BL13)	
		00000004		2920 (BL13) 3825 (BL14) 3831 (BL20)	
TEST 002	BR12	00000002		2819 (BL15)	
	MAR12	00000001		3812 (BL17) 4224 (BL19)	
		00004000		3826 (BL2) 4231 (BL25)	

Fig. 9.18 *Package index table example*

Generally, the items of index condition vary with the index number. Also, the 'REMARKS' column notifies necessary precautions in removing or inserting the packages. In the Fig. 9.15 example, two suspected packages (BL2 and BL25) are derived from the index condition.

Table 9.7   *Examples of traffic measurement registration commands format*

Function	Parameter 1 (P1)	Parameter 2 (P2)	Parameter 3 (P3)	Parameter 4 (P4)
TRF	Link A measurement (ALR)	LLNΔ/TLNΔ	0/1 To be measured or not	
	Junctor measurement (JNC)	LLN/TLN	–	
SUT	Registration (REG)	EL: XX ... X Line equipment number	–	–
	Cancel (CCL)	–		
OGT	Registration (REG)	Route specified (RUT)	–	TG: X ... X Route
		Terminating office specified (OFC)	N: X ... X Terminating office code	
	Cancel (CCL)	–	–	–

9.7 Traffic measurement

Traffic measurement is required to confirm that the system is behaving normally, and to obtain data for improving the load balance within the exchange and for expanding the system in the future, and also to confirm that the system behaves as designed under exceptionally heavy traffic.

Traffic measurement in the electronic switching systems has the main characteristic that there is no need for any particular measurement apparatus, since the measurement is performed by processing information within the processor memory. It is also possible to perform sophisticated processing.

The measurement items are broadly classified into the number of calls, traffic density, occupancy rate and detailed recording.

Most traffic measurements are made regularly. Data is recorded in the memory and output upon request. This method is called routine measurement. Some measurements, which require high machine time and/or increased memory space, are activated selectively on demand by suitable command. This method is called special measurement.

9.7.1 On-demand traffic measurement

Examples of the commands used to initiate on-demand traffic measurements are shown in Table 9.7. These commands all specify the range of items for which the measurements must be taken so as to avoid a high volume of output data. They handle the following traffic:

Link traffic: Command TRF activates measurement of A-link or junctor traffic with the network numbers specified.

Subscriber originating/terminating traffic: Originating and terminating traffic for a particular subscriber is separately measured. Command SUT is input together with his line equipment number to activate or cancel the measurement.

Numbers of calls to particular destinations via particular routes: Calls via a specified route are analysed to count the number of calls to each terminating office, or calls to a specified terminating office are analysed to count the number of such calls carried via each route. Command OGT activates one of the above functions with the route number and destination code specified.

Detailed traffic recording: Calls are sampled at the rate specified to record their subscribers and dial information, time sequence of the state transition and equipment numbers concerned with them. The recorded information is processed in an external system to obtain various traffic data. This function is activated by inputting a command together with a sampling rate N.

9.7.2 Traffic measurement items

Number of calls: The number of calls is counted to analyse the traffic flow and survey the grade of service.

Calls can be analysed in terms of:

(i) Their direction: originating, terminating
(ii) Their categories: intraoffice (own-exchange), local toll, international, operator calls, etc.
(iii) Their progress: abandoned calls, calls encountering called subscriber busy, completed calls, etc.

(iv) Use of optional services: e.g. new services such as abbreviated dialling.

To obtain a measure of the service quality, the number of calls lost due to internal blocking in the speech path switching networks and shortage of facilities is also counted.

The number of calls is counted by call counting macros incorporated into the main call processing program. When identifying a call of a particular category, the program invokes the macro to increment the corresponding traffic meter.

Traffic density: The traffic density in a group of speech trunks, miscellaneous trunks, A-links, junctors, subscriber lines, etc., may be measured. The group of such equipment to be observed is scanned at regular intervals to count the number that are operated. Since the information on the state of each equipment is always stored in the memory, it is periodically scanned to count the number of simultaneous calls. Each count is added into a counter. Since it is assumed that the scanning interval should be the average holding time for the equipment to be observed, or less, the following intervals are used:

> 3 min for speech trunks and the like
> 20 s for miscellaneous trunks.

For example, assume that 1 h observation of a 10-trunk group at 3 min intervals (scanning 20 times) yields a count of 140 calls. The traffic density in the group during the 1 hour is:

$$140 \div 20 \ = \ 7 \text{ (in erlangs)}$$

and the occupancy of the group is $0\cdot7$ ($7 \div 10 = 0\cdot7$).

Measurement of the traffic density is accomplished by particular application programs, such as trunk traffic, A-link traffic and subscriber originating-terminating traffic measuring programs, which are grouped into the administration program. The trunk traffic measuring program, which measures the traffic density in outgoing trunks (OGT) and miscellaneous trunks, is initiated at intervals of 3 min/20 s by the execution control program (B-level controller), and traces the trunk idle chain of each trunk group (TGN) to count the number of idle trunks in the group (the trunk class is used as the trunk scanning interval indicator). The program then subtracts the number of idle trunks from the number of installed trunks belonging to the corresponding TGN to obtain the number of trunks occupied and accumulates the data in the corresponding counter.

This program has an alarm function in addition to the traffic measurement function. When detecting all-busy of a final trunk group 3 times or more within a stated time period, it issues a minor (MN) alarm and outputs an alarm message through the teletypewriter unit.

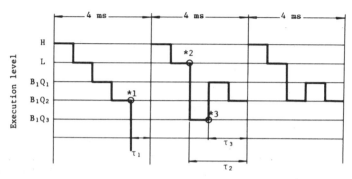

Fig. 9.19   *CC usage rate computation*

   *1: Add the residue of the 4 ms at the completion of all the B_1Q_2 tasks

   *2: When a B_1Q_3 task or lower, which has been interrupted in the foregoing 4 ms is resumed, add the residue of the present 4 ms

   *3: When the interrupted B_1Q_3 task or lower is completed, subtract the residue of the present 4 ms

Usage rate: The usage rate of the central control (CC) is measured by a particular program which is initiated every 20 s. The usage rate of a speech path controller (SC and RC), transaction record or other specified memory block is measured by a particular program which is initiated at 1 s intervals. The CC usage rate is measured by the execution control program. The program accounts the CC time consumed, within a time period (20 s), in executing programs of level B_1Q_2 or higher and obtains the usage rate which is defined as the ratio of the used time above to the total time period. As seen from Fig. 9.19, the CC usage rate in the 20 s time period is calculated as follows:

$$n(\text{CC usage rate}) = \left(1 - \sum_{20\,s} (T_1 + T_2 - T_3)/20 \times 10^3\right) \times 100\%$$

This measurement has immediate control over the processor. The usage rate is compared with reference values α, β and γ, shown in Fig. 9.20, and if they are exceeded the program stops the speech path test and issues an alarm.

Detailed traffic recording: For statistical purposes, the complete details of every Nth call are recorded onto magnetic tape. This information includes a time of origination, directory number, status number, task number and dialled information, and is recorded every time the call undergoes a state transition. This detailed traffic information is processed by an external system to provide useful data, such as traffic for each destination, holding time distribution, state probability and state transition probability.

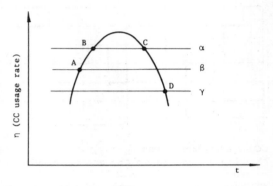

A: Suspend of speech path test

B: CC usage rate over alarm

C: Cancel CC usage rate over alarm

D: Restore speech path test omission

Fig. 9.20   *Traffic control using CC usage rate*

Traffic measurement output: Measured traffic data are accumulated in a buffer area of the main memory (TM) except for detailed traffic information. They are transferred to the buffer area in the magnetic drum every hour. After the transfer, the buffer area in TM is cleared to provide for the next hour's traffic data. The transfer start time can be specified by a command. Once the time is specified, the transfer starts at the same time every hour. The buffer area in the magnetic drum has a capacity for 12 h of traffic data; when new data arrive, they replace old data transferred 12 h before.

Traffic data recorded on the magnetic drum are output onto the magnetic tape or to a teletypewriter unit as specified by command parameters which can also specify 1 or 12 h traffic data for routine or special measurement.

The detailed traffic measurement starts at the command input to record the collected information onto magnetic tape.

9.8 Observation

The purpose of observation is to collect data with a view to improving the service quality. It is classified into service grade observation and charge meter observation.

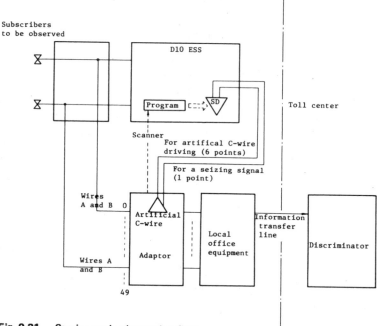

Fig. 9.21 *Service grade observation flow*

9.8.1 *Service grade observation*

A centralised observation system has been introduced into the Japanese telephone network; it aims at the collection of data on the switching performance and subscriber behaviour. This system consists of a discriminator installed in a toll centre (trunk exchange) and local office equipment installed in an end office. Subscriber lines to be observed are extended to the local office equipment from the exchange. The equipment selects one from among simultaneous calls to connect it to the discriminator. The latter monitors and identifies dialled digits, tone signals, answer signal, voice current, etc., to determine the process of the call completion, incompletion due to busy or no answer, nonconnection due to a trouble, etc. It then outputs the results in a format convenient for computer processing.

The local office equipment is initiated through wire C (the third wire) provided for each subscriber. The electronic exchange, which does not have such a control wire, simulates the C wire by providing an adaptor controlled through the signal distributor (SD), as shown in Fig. 9.21.

The service grade observation therefore requires the following processing:

(i) Registration/cancellation of the subscribers to be observed

(ii) Local office equipment start/release.

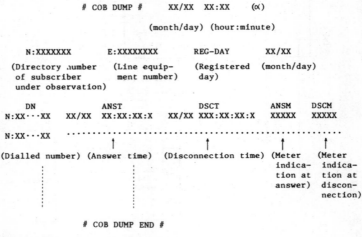

Fig. 9.22   *Charge observation information output format*

9.8.2 Charge meter observation

Billing systems may be classified into detailed record systems and bulk billing systems. In the former system, detailed charge information, including calling and called subscriber numbers and call conversation start and end times, is recorded for each call. In the latter, only the cumulative total of the charges is recorded for each subscriber.

In Japan the latter method is used for normal billing purposes but a charge observation feature is provided to record detailed charge information on subscribers who complain about their charges. The electronic switching system realises the features by registration/cancellation functions for subscribers to be observed, collecting charge information on all calls from them, transferring it to a file in the magnetic drum and outputting the accumulated data in the file upon request from the maintenance engineer. The output format of the data is shown in Fig. 9.22.

9.9 Service order processing

The electronic switching system holds data on each subscriber on the magnetic drum. The subscriber data consist of *the originating line translation word*, which is indexed with the line equipment number to specify the originating class of service, and *the terminating line translation word*, which is indexed with the directory number to specify terminating class of service. In the electronic switching system, as seen from this, correspondence between directory number and line equipment number can be determined by translation of originating and terminating line words without any restriction. This is in contrast to a crossbar exchange, where the translator (called a number group) is the hardware equivalent to only the terminating line translation word and therefore imposes considerable restrictions on telephone number or line equipment number selection. This lack of limitation in an ESS provides a high flexibility to responding to subscribers' needs.

In a crossbar exchange, subscriber changes which occur daily require physical rewiring within the number group. In the electronic exchange, this operation is replaced by rewriting subscriber data on the magnetic drum. The subscriber data rewriting (called service order processing) is made by inputting a service order command followed by service order in the form of paper tape or magnetic tape through the teletypewriter unit or magnetic tape unit. To simplify the confirmation of the correct subscriber data change and for subscriber data administration, the system is provided with a data read function to systematically output the subscriber data in the magnetic drum through the teletypewriter unit.

9.9.1 Subscriber data format

Subscriber data consists of originating and terminating line translation tables together with auxiliary blocks and variable abbreviated dialling and multiline hunting group lists. The general organisation is shown in Fig. 9.23.

The origination line translation table is provided in blocks which provide 2048 translations each. Each translation consists of 2 words which normally provide the originating class of service plus the directory number. The starting address of particular table to be used is obtained from a 128-entry primary table indexed by the most significant 7 bits of the LEN. The entry within the translation table is obtained by indexing by the remaining 11 bits of the LEN. The reason for the two-stage table is to remove the need to provide memory space for the maximum number of lines in a partially-equipped system.

The terminating line translation tables are of similar format except that each of the tables are provided for 1000 numbers.

The two-word information area is sufficient for most of subscribers, but additional space is required for party-line, abbreviated dialling service and multiline hunting group subscribers. This additional area is provided by an auxiliary block and abbreviated dialling and multiline hunting group lists which are linked to their translation words.

Fig. 9.24 *a* and *b* show parts of data fields in the originating and terminating line translation words and their meaning.

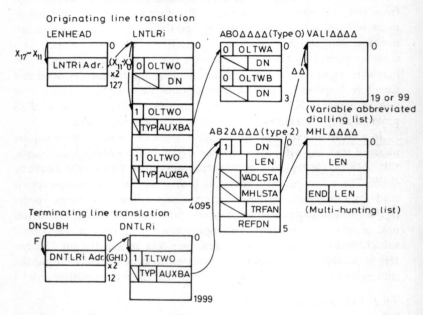

Fig. 9.23   *Subscriber data memory linkage*

9.9.2 Service order processing flow
To process a relatively small number of daily changes, their *service order forms* are punched on paper tape by the maintenance engineer and input through the teletypewriter. When handling a large number of changes for an extension their service order forms are recorded on magnetic tape by the subscriber data conversion program in the software centre (see Chapter 12). After this they are input through the magnetic tape unit. Fig. 9.25 shows the service order processing flow.

Kinds of service orders
The example of the service orders used in the electronic exchange are:

(*a*) *New registration:* New subscriber is registered. New class of service can also be registered simultaneously.

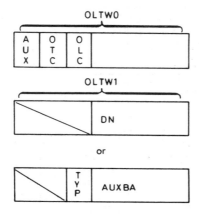

Symbol	Designation	Value	Meaning
OLTW0	Originating translation word 0		
AUX	Auxiliary block	0 1	None Present
OTC	Originating terminal class	0 0 0 0 0 1 0 1 0 . . .	Vacant terminal Ordinary Originating test terminal
OLC	Originating line class	0 1	Local line Centrex line
. . .	. . .	. . .	. . .
OLTW1	Originating translation word 1		
DN	Directory number		
TYP	Auxiliary block type		
AUXBA	Auxiliary block address		

Fig. 9.24 *Data structure for line translation word*
a Originating

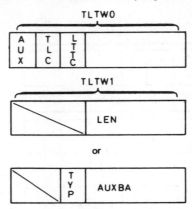

Symbol	Designation	Value	Meaning
TLTW0	Terminating translation word 0		
AUX	Auxiliary block	0 1	None Present
TLC	LS terminating line class	0 0 0 1 1 0 1 1	Special terminating line Local line Centrex line (Spare)
LTLC	LS terminating line class	0 0 0 0 0 1 0 1 0 0 1 1 1 0 0 . . .	Individual line Party-line A Party-line B Multi-hunting group . . . .
.	.	.	
.	.	.	
.	.	.	
TLTW1	Terminating translation word 1		
LEN	Line equipment number		
TYP	Auxiliary block type		
AUXBA	Auxiliary block address		

b Terminating

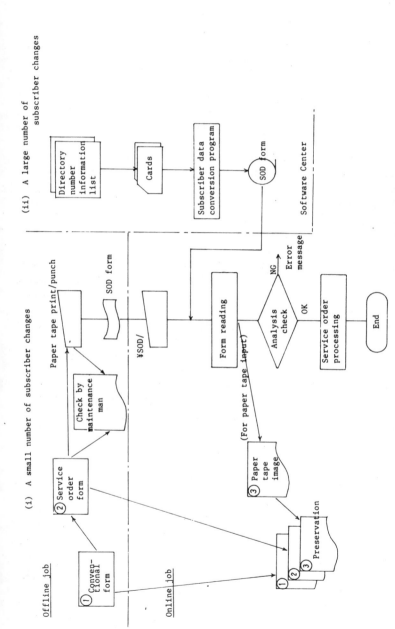

Fig. 9.25 *Service order processing flow*

(*b*) *New multiline hunting group registration:* New subscription for a multiline hunting group is registered.

(*c*) *Multiline hunting group addition:* New lines are registered to add them to an existing multiline hunting group.

(*d*) *New service registration:* New services requested by existing subscribers are registered newly or additionally.

(*e*) *Party-line subscriber registration:* A party-line subscriber is registered.

(*f*) *Subscriber class change:* A party-line subscription is changed to an individual subscriber.

(*g*) *Number change:* A directory number is changed to another number available within the same switching unit. Calls terminating at the old number will be intercepted by automatic intercept system (see next Chapter).

(*h*) *Multiline hunting group number change:* Directory numbers, including a pilot number are changed.

(*i*) *Line equipment number change:* A line equipment number of an individual subscriber is changed.

(*j*) *Multiline hunting group line equipment number change:* Line equipment numbers of a multiline hunting group, including a pilot number are changed.

Service order program arrangement and processing flow

The service order program consists of the service order analysis and service order processing programs. The service order processing consists of functional modules arranged as part of the command processor described earlier.

Fig. 9.26 shows the service order processing flow. When a service order command (¥SOD) is input, the command analysis initiates the service-order analysis. The analysis then reads the service order from data on paper tape or magnetic tape, assembles them into a format suitable for the following service order processing, and transfers necessary information (subscriber data, charge meter, etc.) from the magnetic drum to a transaction record. The command analysis selects the command units necessary for processing the order and turns over the address of the command unit table to the command execution controller. The controller hands over control to an element after transferring it from the magnetic drum to the overlay area in accordance with the designation of the unit table. When the element execution is completed, control is returned to the command execution controller, which in turn retrieves the next element from the unit table to repeat the same processing as above. The command end element is finally executed before terminating the command processing.

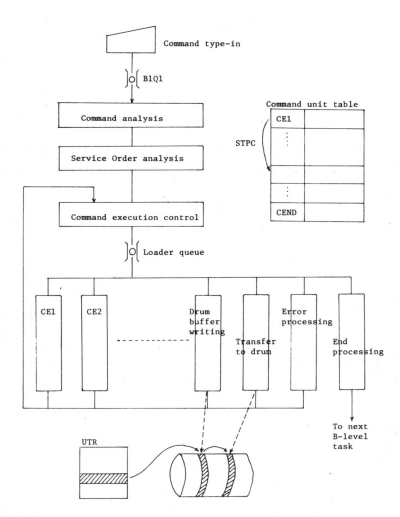

Fig. 9.26 *Service order program arrangement*

Chapter 10

Programming of special services

In the previous Section, switching programs were classified into several groups, such as call processing programs, administrative programs and the like. Each of these programs was explained on the basis of describing the functions of its individual program, such as line supervisory scanning program, digit analysis program, etc. This Chapter shows how these are assembled to form a specific feature by giving some typical examples of features.

10.1 Variable abbreviated dialling (VAD) service

The variable abbreviated dialling (VAD) feature is a service which allows subscribers to assign a short code (VAD code) to represent certain frequently called numbers, and permits them to dial the selected dial numbers using fewer digits than normally required. The subscribers can assign or change VAD codes at will by operating their own telephone set.

Three items are necessary for this service

(a) VAD class registration
(b) VAD code registration
(c) VAD code dialling.

10.1.1 VAD class registration

As stated in Chapter 9, there are two classes of service defined for each subscriber, the line equipment number translation (LNTLR) word for outgoing calls and the directory number translation (DNTLR) word for incoming calls. For the VAD service, a flag (VAD flag) is defined within the LNTLR word, which shows whether or not the associated subscriber is allowed the service. In addition, a memory block called a variable abbreviated dial list (VADLST) for storing the abbreviated dial information must be linked to the LNTLR word via an auxiliary block, as shown in the Fig. 10.1.

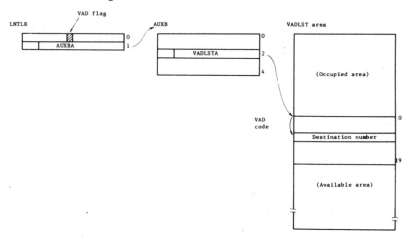

Fig. 10.1 *LNTLR, AUXB and VADLST for VAD service*

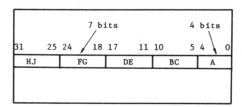

Note; For a local call, 0 is stored in the A field to
discriminate the local number from the toll number

Fig. 10.2 *VADLST format for dialled code AB . . . J*

Any subscriber who wants the VAD service has to be 'registered' in the LNTLR word to be qualified for using the service. At a subscriber's request for the VAD service, the maintenance engineer inputs a service order command via the teletypewriter unit. The service order program, instructed by the command, reads the subscriber number out of the command parameters, and activates the VAD flag in the LNTLR word associated with the subscriber. Then, it obtains the necessary memory space (20 words for each subscriber) out of the auxiliary memory block area and allocates it for the VADLST linking with the LNTLR.

Fig. 10.2 shows the VADLST format. Normally, each digit requires four bits in binary coded decimal code. A total of 36 bits (4 bits × 9 digits) would be necessary for storing a national number. Actually, however, dialled codes are taken two at a time and coded into 7 bits each. This allows 8 digits to be stored in 28 bits and the initial digit is stored in 4 bits. Thus the code is packed into one word (32 bits) with the result of saving the memory space required for the VADLST.

10.1.2 VAD code registration

To use the VAD service, the qualified subscriber must assign a 2-digit VAD code to a number and register it in the VADLST. For this, the dialling sequence is

$$\underbrace{0*}_{(1)} + \underbrace{\Delta\Delta}_{(2)} + \underbrace{XXX - X}_{(3)}$$

Note: (1) Special code for VAD registration
       (2) VAD code assigned to the destination number (10 to 29)
       (3) Destination number to be stored.

As explained in Chapter 6, the pretranslation program, activated at 100 ms intervals, analyses the digits that are stored in the ORM by the digit storing program. On analysing the first two digits (0*) of the dialled numbers, the pretranslation program identifies the call to be for 'VAD registration' and determines both the digit block string number (DBSN) given to the call and the length of digits to be received (see Chapter 6). When all the digits are received, it hunts for an available hopper transaction memory block (HPTR), stores in it necessary information required for further processing, such as the starting address of the program to follow, the process identifier (SID) to show the course of processing, the originating register trunk number (ORTN) to linkage with the ORM, and so on. Then, it attaches the HPTR at the base level queue. The other necessary information, such as the dialled number, the DBSN, etc., are stored in the ORM.

When, later, the base level control program detaches the HPTR from the queue, control is transferred to the digit analysis program as specified by the address information previously stored in the HPTR. The digit analysis program then takes control of the VAD registration process. In this process, the digit analysis program identifies the call to be a VAD registration call by the DBSN in the ORM and checks whether or not the originating subscriber is allowed the service by referring to the VAD flag in the LNTLR. If service is allowable, the task number and next state number are determined by looking up the task decision tables.

Fig. 10.3 illustrates a VAD registration processing flow in the 'task' determined. In this task, 'task macros' NESR and JOBEX are responsible for VAD registration processing. NESR converts the destination number in the ORM into the special VADLST form, as described above, and stores the converted digits in the *call processing transaction memory block* (CPTR) with additional necessary information, such as the write address in the drum memory, digits $* + \Delta\Delta$ in the service trunk memory block (SVM) to be used later for a verification purpose. Next, JOBEX attaches the CPTR at the queue for transferring the CPTR to the drum IOCS program.

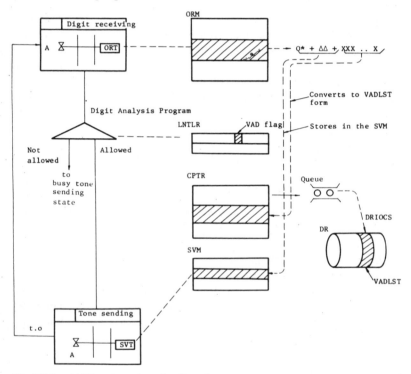

Fig. 10.3   *VAD code registration flowchart*
t.o. time out

After completion of this task, the subscriber is informed of his correct operation by hearing an acceptance tone produced by the next state. Moreover, if the subscriber stays on the line in this tone sending state for a certain length of time (4 to 5 s), he will be connected automatically to the dialled destination subscriber, which enables him to confirm whether or not the dialled VAD code is exactly identical to the number entered. This verification processing is almost the same as when the subscriber dials the VAD code (see next Section), because, as mentioned before, the VAD code (∗ + ΔΔ) where previously stored in the SVM and they can be regarded as having originally been dialled and stored in the ORM.

10.1.3 VAD code dialling

When the subscriber wishes to use the VAD service, the only operation is to dial the special code ∗ plus the VAD code ΔΔ. All the succeeding processes are almost the same as in registration until the digit analysis program takes control. The digit analysis program reads the VADLST associated with the subscriber from the drum memory, converts the digits in VADLST form into an ordinary destination number and stores the data in the ORM. Subsequent processing is exactly the same as that of an ordinary outgoing processing, because the originating subscriber can be considered as having originally dialled the ordinary destination number.

10.2 International subscriber dialling service (ISD)

For ISD service, the subscriber is required to dial

$$\underbrace{00}_{(1)} + \underbrace{X}_{(2)} + \underbrace{XX}_{(3)} \quad \underbrace{X + XX \longrightarrow X}_{(4)}$$

Note: (1) International access code
(2) Service class code
X = 1 for a subscriber dialled call
X = 2 for a charge information service call (in Japanese)
X = 3 for a charge information service call (in English)
X = 4 for an operator assistance call
X = 5 for an information service call
(3) Country number
(4) Domestic number

Fig. 10.4 shows a trunking diagram for a domestic and international exchange network. ISD calls are first centralised at one of the two domestic gateway switches through the domestic exchange network and then are routed to the international gateway switch (INTS).

Fig. 10.5 shows the signalling method between the local exchange

(LS) and the international gateway switch. First, a connection is established between the local system and the international system on a link-by-link basis and then the originating subscriber number and the dialled number (service class code plus country number plus domestic number) are sent on the end-to-end basis, both by means of multifrequency signalling systems.

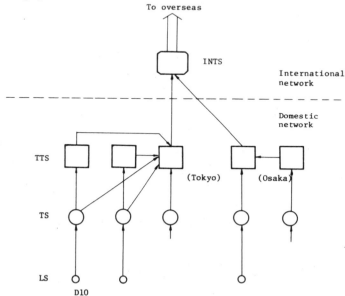

Fig. 10.4 *ISD trunking diagram*
TTS Trunk transit switch
TS   Toll switch
LS   Local switch

The originating subscriber number is used for charge recording at the INTS.[*] For a system other than the stored program control system, it is a somewhat difficult technique to transmit the originating subscriber number to an outgoing call connection and send it to another exchange. A crossbar system usually requires some additional facilities for this purpose. In the D-10 system, however, the originating subscriber number is originally contained in the LNTLR, and a program can determine it at any time when required by simply reading out the LNTLR from the drum memory, which enables the D-10 system easily providing the above facilities.

[*] Editor's note: In Japan the international system is provided by a separate company, the KDD, who determine the charge for the calls.

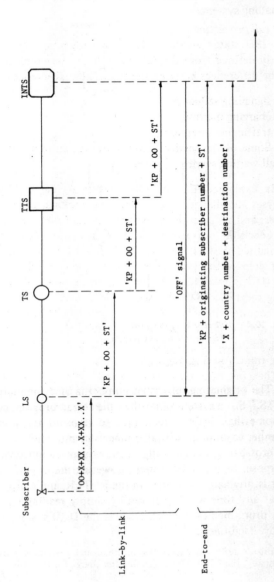

Fig. 10.5 Signalling method between LS and INTS

ISD class registration

Subscribers need to be 'registered' in the LNTLR to use the ISD service. A flag (INT flag) is defined in the LNTLR for this purpose. The INT flag is registered in the LNTLR by the maintenance engineer inputting the service order command.

ISD call processing

The ISD state-transition diagrams, shown in Fig. 10.6, are independently defined from that of the ordinary outgoing connection because of the differences between the two. These differences are:

(*a*) signalling sequence
(*b*) charging method
(*c*) traffic measurement
(*d*) Some of the service features are not allowed for the ISD call, such as call waiting service.

As explained in detail in Chapter 6, the digit analysis program analyses the dialled ISD number, by looking up the digit translation tables, and, as a result, gets necessary data required for the succeeding task decision processing and task execution. This data includes the normalised destination code (DSC) and the trunk group number. The next step is the task decision processing, in which, as shown in the Fig. 10.7, is involved looking up the tree-structured 'task decision tables' using the table index data (i.e. DBSN, DSC and INT flag), and finding the required information of the next state number (NSTN) and the task number (TSN), at the final table. The Figure illustrates that the next status number is 56 and the task number is 0 (refer to the ISD state transition diagram in Fig. 10.6).

The control is now transferred to the task execution control program to execute the 'task' that has been determined by the digit analysis program. As described in detail in Chapter 6, each task is associated with a table called a 'task table', in which a number of programs called 'task macros' are listed and sequentially activated by the task execution control program to perform a specific task. In the above task for an ISD call, a total of about 30 task macros are required. Some of the typical task macros are illustrated as follows:

(*a*) *LTSC macro* to select an outgoing trunk and find a speech path between a subscriber and the outgoing trunk
(*b*) *TTSC macro* to select an outgoing sender trunk and find a speech path between the outgoing trunk and the outgoing sender trunk
(*c*) *OGTE macro and OSTE macro* to edit the trunk control commands

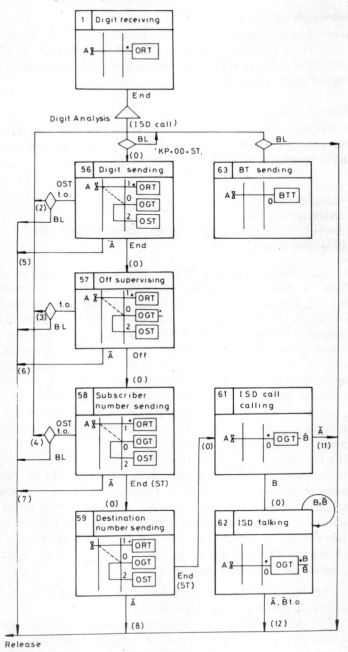

Fig. 10.6   *ISD call state-transition diagram*

and speech path connection commands in the call processing transaction memory block (CPTR)

(*d*) *LINK macro* to link all trunk memory blocks with each other and store the next state number (56) in the trunk memory blocks

(*e*) *JOBEX macro* to attach the CPTR at a queue

(*f*) *TMTS macro* to deactivate a timer for digits reception

(*g*) *SMCU macro* to activate a control bit for supervising the subscriber

(*h*) *DSC macro* to arrange digits to be sent forward in the outgoing sender trunk memory block

(*i*) *TRF macro* to count ISD call traffic

Plus others.

When all these tasks are executed, the call moves to state 56 (digit sending), where the line connection signals, KP + 00 + ST, are sent forward to a trunk exchange, as shown in Fig. 10.6. The call finally reaches state 62 (ISD talking state) to begin a conversation with an overseas subscriber.

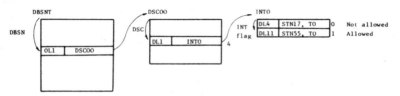

Fig. 10.7   *Task decision tables*

Digit sending

The ISD call digit-sending method is significantly different from that of an ordinary outgoing call, in regard to the following two points.

(*a*) The digits are sent by the end-to-end signalling method, not by the link-by-link method, because the maximum number of digits to be sent to INTS reaches as many as 20 digits and exceeds the capacity of the digit receiving and sending facilities in the conventional trunk exchanges.

(*b*) Two state-transition diagrams are separately defined for digit sending, that is, the subscriber number sending state and the destination number sending state, because the outgoing sender trunk memory (OSM) has insufficient space for storing both the subscriber number and the destination number.

10.3 Automatic intercept service (AIS)

Automatic intercept service is a feature which enables calls, which are directed to an improper telephone number such as a 'changed number', a 'disconnected number' etc., to receive an announcement service automatically by a voice announcement generating system.

Fig. 10.8 shows a block diagram for the AIS system. All AIS calls, which are directed to local exchanges in a given area, are directed to the AIS centre through the AIS trunk line. They are answered by a specified vocal announcement according to the type of call made. The AIS centre consists of four major facilities; incoming trunk circuits, a connection network, an audio magnetic drum memory and a control system including a magnetic drum memory. Many vocal segments are recorded in the audio magnetic drum memory. The AIS system reassembles them into a meaningful announcement.

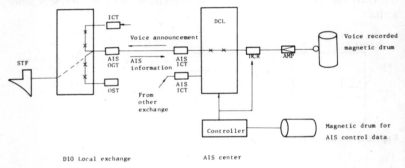

Fig. 10.8 *AIS service-tracking diagram*

10.3.1 AIS classes and AIS address
Two kinds of service classes are defined in the DNTLR word in relation to the AIS service, i.e. the terminating service mode (TSM) class and the special terminating (STC) class, as shown in Fig. 10.9. Each of these classes consists of 4 bits in the DNTLR word. 0101 (in binary) of the TSM class and 0011 (in binary) of the STC class are assigned to the 'disconnected number' and the 'changed number', respectively. In addition, the DNTLR also includes the AIS address, as shown in the Figure. The AIS address gives the logical address of the memory block in the magnetic drum memory at the AIS centre, in which the 'AIS control data' are stored for assembling the 'vocal segments' to form a complete AIS voice announcement. The AIS classes and the AIS address are input into the DNTLR word by a service order command.

Writing AIS control data
AIS control data is written into the magnetic drum memory at the AIS
centre by the remote control of a maintenance engineer at the local
exchange. First, the maintenance engineer inputs the AIS command via
a teletypewriter unit, for example of changed number, ¥AIS (AIS
mode), (write address), (old telephone number), (new telephone number)/, which are temporarily stored in some memory block. Then, he
operates various keys on the supervisory test frame (STF) to establish
a communication line between the local exchange and the AIS centre
and sends the stored AIS control data to the AIS centre through the
established line. When these data are received and written correctly in
the magnetic drum memory, an acknowledgment signal is sent back to
the STF.

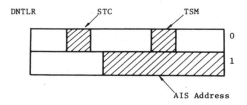

Fig. 10.9 *AIS service classes and AIS address data in the DNTLR*

AIS call connection
Fig. 10.10 shows the AIS service state-transition diagrams. After digits
reception is completed, the digit analysis program analyses the digits.
When it determines that it is an incoming call to be terminated, the
terminating line analysis program is called. The terminating line analysis
program reads the DNTLR word, which is corresponded to the received
directory number, out of the magnetic drum memory, analyses the call,
using various data, such as the output data of the digit analysis program
and the classes of service in the DNTLR word, and finally determines
the task number and the next state number. Then, the task execution
control program executes the chosen task (87-0 or 87-1). Various task
macros sequentially work to perform the task, similar to those described
in Section 10.2. For instance, the DSC macro stores the AIS address
data in the outgoing sender trunk memory (OSM). The AIS data was
previously transferred from the DNTLR word into the task execution
working memory block (TEM) by the terminating line analysis program,
as shown in Fig. 10.10.

After completion of the AIS task (call in state 22 or state 26,

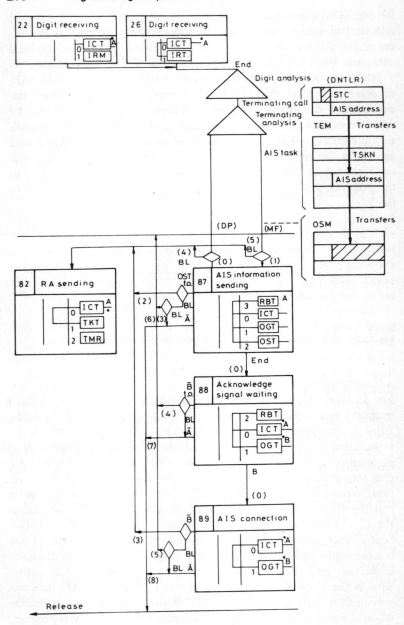

Fig. 10.10 *AIS call state-transition diagram*
RA Recorded announcement

depending on the signalling type of the incoming call), the call moves to state 87, where the AIS address data is sent to the AIS centre through an outgoing trunk while a ring back tone is sent back to the origination subscriber through the incoming trunk.

The call is now in state 88, where it waits for an answer signal and, on receiving the answer signal, the call finally reaches the AIS connection state (89), where the incoming trunk is connected through to the AIS centre and the AIS voice announcement is sent back from the AIS centre to the originating subscriber through the line established by the process described.

10.4 Overload control

Exchange traffic has considerable randomly varying characteristics, such as varying from time to time and concentrating in some specific period, i.e. at some hour in a day, in some day in a month, and in some season in a year. Taking this traffic characteristic into consideration, a switching system is generally so designed as to have a full capacity to service the normal peak traffic.

However, occasionally an exceptionally heavy traffic caused by some social event or natural calamity happens. An overload can also occur after one of the system restart phases which has denied calling detection for a short period. Hence a switching system must be provided with 'overload control facilities', in which it detects these exeptional circumstances as soon as possible and takes some proper actions to keep itself in a normal condition for switching services. A stored program control system is fully flexible to be easily and effectively provided with the overload control facilities.

The requirements for designing an automatic overload control mechanism are:

(*a*) that it should be as simple as possible
(*b*) the regulation should be restricted to calls causing the overload
(*c*) the effects of congestion should not be allowed to spread over the network
(*d*) the regulation process should not impose a large load on the central control
(*e*) unaccepted calls should not impose a load on the control
(*f*) whenever the overload traffic condition disappears, the system should revert immediately to normal working.

10.4.1 Overload detection
The D-10 system provides three kinds of overload detection facilities.

(i) *Call origination overload*

As described in Chapter 5, scanning of subscribers' lines is performed by the program. When this program detects a call origination, it hunts for an available transaction memory block (HPTR) and connects it to the queue to transfer the necessary information to the originating line analysis program. As the call origination traffic increases, the scanning program and other output processing programs will consume increasing amounts of the real time of a central processor. At some stage there will be inadequate central processor time for the base level programs to promptly handle the detected calls. Thus, the length of the HPTR queue increases and the number of available HPTRs becomes less. Under these conditions, some of the originating calls will encounter HPTR blockage and, as a result, are forced to wait until the next scanning cycle before they are detected. This mechanism therefore automatically smooths very temporary peaks of traffic. If the origination overload is maintained, the line supervisory scanning program detects that in a significant number of subsequent scans it is unable to process all the calls. In this case an emergency action is instigated which takes calling conditions from nonpriority subscribers and puts them into the high and dry (H & D) state. Those subscribers in the H & D state are then locked out and have no effect at all upon the line supervisory scanning program.

The subscriber lines set in the H & D state are placed under the control of an H & D supervisory program which is activated nominally every 10 s. This program examines the line loops of those subscribers in the H & D and if no loop is detected the subscriber is restored to the idle state. This program however is executed at the lowest level of priority ($B_1 Q_3$) so that the frozen lines are restored gradually as a function of spare processing time.

In prolonged extreme overload (i.e. one lasting for minutes rather than seconds) the H & D process can in fact spread congestion through the network as calls incoming to a H & D subscriber will receive busy tone. For this reason a secondary overload control mechanism must be provided whereby the power supply to a predetermined proportion of the circuits is removed. This now prevents a calling condition but permits a terminating call.

(ii) *Specific route congestion*

It sometimes happens that there is a high concentration of outgoing calls to a specific route while general traffic conditions remain normal. Typically this can occur after a disaster is reported in some area of the country and people ring into that area to obtain information. This condition is not desirable as it will cause congestion in the total telephone network and should be detected as soon as possible. For this purpose a special program is provided which regularly monitors the 'main routes' conditions and requests an alarm message to be typed out when it detects some route to be overloaded so that a maintenance engineer can input command to modify the routing of calls to that area. A typical countermeasure is to connect a proportion of calls to a suitable recorded announcement instructing the caller to call an operator if the call is urgent.

(iii) *Central control overload*

It is usually necessary for the central control to keep some reserve of capacity so that even in the most congested traffic hour it may withstand possible intermittent peak traffic. Therefore, the average processor occupancy percentage must be controlled to prevent it exceeding some threshold level. One of the traffic measurement programs is assigned for measuring the central control occupancy. The program is located at the lowest level, i.e. $B_1 Q_3$, in the program execution priority hierarchy and measures the total execution time consumed by $B_1 Q_3$ programs. The 'effective' central control occupancy can be defined as the proportion of time (over some period) for which programs at a level higher than $B_1 Q_3$ occupy the central processor because no call processing programs are placed in this lowest $B_1 Q_3$ level and $B_1 Q_3$ programs never hold the central control while some call processing remains to be performed.

When the program determines that the central control occupancy exceeds a predetermined threshold level, it sends alarms to cause the maintenance engineer to take appropriate actions.

Some examples of the various overload conditions and the actions taken are given in Table 10.1.

Table 10.1 *Overload detection and action*

	Detection	Action
Route congestion	Certain route was busy for three consecutive times when a monitor program tries every 20 s or 3 min, depending on the routes.	The maintenance man inputs commands to restrict some subscribers classed to a low priority from going to the congested route, or start up the 'variable routing' facility to rearrange the routing scheme.
	Minor alarms (audible and visible) are output together with a message on the teletypewriter unit.	
Call origination overload	Subscriber line scanning can not be completed for two consecutive cycles (0·4 s), because of the HPTR blockage.	(a) The line supervisory scanning program makes the 'minor call restriction mode' effective, in which public telephones are normally connected and ordinary telephones are restricted. If an ordinary telephone attempts a call origination, he is compelled to be a 'H & D' state, which makes the subscriber line electrically disconnected from the system until the program makes the mode ineffective.
	Major alarms (audible and visible) and a message are output.	Incoming calls are normally connected to subscribers.
		(b) The maintenance man also takes some proper action.

Table 10.1 *contd.,*

	Detection	Action
Central control overload	(i) More than 95% occupancy of the central control continues for more than 20 s.	The central control occupancy measuring program makes the 'major call restriction mode' effective, in which public telephones are normally connected, but ordinary subscriber line relays are cut off so that they can not attempt any call origination. Incoming calls are normally connected to any subscribers.
	Major alarms and a message are output.	The maintenance man can also make the mode effective by a command and key operations on the STF any time as occasion arises.
	(ii) The central control occupancy reached threshold level n, m, x, and y. The value n, m, x and y are programmable by a command.	Various routine tests and some low priority processings are skipped according to the various threshold levels.

Chapter 11

Program file structure

The previous chapters outline individual parts of the complete switching program. This and the next Chapter describe how the complete program system is produced and managed and the necessary management tools and the type of problems that occur in program system management.

The word 'file' is used to refer to a block of information which has been systematically structured so as to serve a particular purpose. A program file is a file whose purpose is to govern the sequence of execution of a number of different processing steps. For the purpose of management, a program file is often stored in a nonvolatile medium, such as magnetic tape. Once a magnetic tape has been committed to the storage of such information and labelled accordingly, it may be considered to be a program file.

11.1 Generic structure

One of the important objectives of adopting stored program control of switching system is the ease with which an existing exchange may be modified or have new functions added without any hardware modification work. Therefore, it becomes important to consider how modification or addition of functions can be easily accomplished.

For this purpose of easy software management, the D-10 system program files are designed to have a generic structure which is defined below.

Depending on the local characteristics and the network interface requirements, each exchange system will have a unique personality. Obviously, it would be prohibitively expensive to provide a completely new set of programs for each exchange, but it is equally unacceptable for all exchanges to have to conform to one standard set of programs.

The generic approach provides a compromise solution by permitting all exchanges to share a standard set of software. In addition, each is provided with a unique set of software to satisfy its individual needs.

There are two approaches to providing the generic structured program files for the D-10 system.

11.1.1 Generic structure for office conditions

Exchanges which are ranked at the same stage in the exchange hierarchy (e.g. local stage exchange) can be considered as being almost the same, from the exchange 'function' standpoint, but are different in regard to office 'condition', such as various traffic conditions, the number of the lines and trunks, the numbering scheme, and so on.

The first approach to the generic structure of the program file is to clearly separate the conditions from the function and thus get the same ranked exchange to have a common set of programs to specify the various switching function and have a different set of data to specify each office condition.

11.1.2 Generic structure for system conditions

The differently ranked exchanges (e.g. local exchanges, trunk exchanges, etc.) are different from each other in regard to their main functions but still have some commonality in various points, such as administrative features, fault processing function and even some call processing functions.

The second approach to the generic structure is to integrate the total exchange function into one program file set called a MOTHER FILE, including some differences between the different exchange systems and thus enables the program file to be easily managed.

The second approach, which requires more sophisticated techniques, is discussed in Chapter 13. This Chapter discusses the techniques of separating program from data.

11.2 Separation of data from program

The first step towards a generic structure is to separate the programs, which specify the function, from the data, which define individual characteristics of an exchange.

As an example, let us take the case where some program counts clock periods until the count reaches some predetermined value. In this case, even if the counting value is known, it is not specified in the program but is declared as a separate parameter, as shown in the Fig. 11.1.

The program simply counts the clock periods until the count reaches the value specified by the parameter.

These parameters can be divided into two categories:

(i) *System parameters* which are not dependent on the particular exchange

(ii) *Office parameters*, which may vary from exchange (office) to exchange.

These parameters are usually implemented in the program by a separate data block and are referred to as *system dependent data* or *office dependent data*, as appropriate.

Once the program and the system-dependent data are designed for the specific exchange system, they are only changed when there is some system modification. Therefore, their combination is called a *system file*.

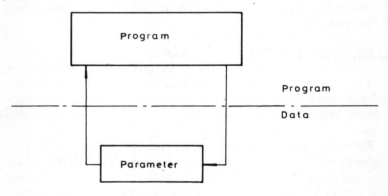

Fig. 11.1 *Program separation from data*

Office data structure

Office data depends on individual office conditions, which may vary from office to office and further vary from time to time as the exchange grows. Therefore, the office data structure is designed to be fully flexible for variations as regards both the contents of the data and the volume of data.

Fig. 11.2 shows a typical office data structure. As shown in the Figure, a number of tables are formed and are chained to each other. Apart from the primary table, the remaining tables may be located anywhere in memory. The objective information is stored in the final table. Programs can access this information by tracing the table chain with an access parameter. Each of the tables is called, in sequence, 'primary

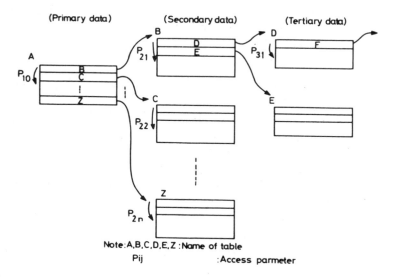

Note: A,B,C,D,E,Z : Name of table
Pij : Access parmeter

Fig. 11.2   *Office data structure*

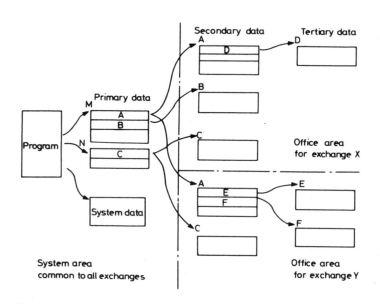

Fig. 11.3   *Memory allocation*

data', 'secondary data', 'tertiary data' and so on, according to its degree in the chain. The number of degrees and the size of each of the tables depend on the type of office data.

Fig. 11.3 shows office data memory allocation. The primary data is allocated in the system area, together with the program and system data, and this has the special purpose of making the office data relocatable to enable easy data expansion. The system area is common in the size and location in the memory to all exchanges, while the office area varies with each of the exchanges, as shown in the Figure.

Fig. 11.4 shows an actual example of the tree-structured office data. It illustrates that the objective data, RCN (i.e. relay address in a relay controller), can be found in the secondary data or tertiary data with the access parameter, TN (i.e. trunk number).

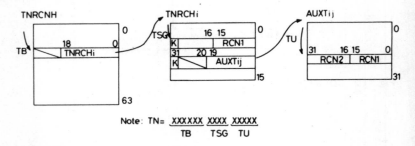

Fig. 11.4   *Example of actual office data*
(TN → RCN translation table)

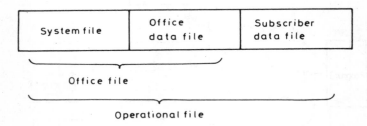

Fig. 11.5   *File structure*

11.3 File structure and management

11.3.1 General

Fig. 11.5 shows the D-10 system file structure. The *system file* is defined as a collection of program and system data and commonly used to

Table 11.1

	Generated		Managed	
	at	by	at	by
System file	Software centre	Language processor	Software centre	Language processor and Update system
Office file	Software centre	Office data generator	Software centre in the case of major change	Office data generator and Office parameter re-generator
			or exchange site in the case of minor change	Command program for data change and ex-pansion test
Subscriber data table	Software centre at cut over or big scale expansion	Subscriber data generator	—	—
	or exchange site	Command program (Service order program)	Exchange site	Command program (Service order program)

all exchanges. The *office data file* is defined as a collection of office data and is to be prepared for each exchange. These two files are combined to be defined as the *office file*. The *subscriber data file* is a collection of the subscriber data. All these are combined and defined as the *operational file*.

These three files differ from each other in their generation and management, as shown in Table 11.1. Fig. 11.6 shows how these files are combined to be supplied to the exchange site.

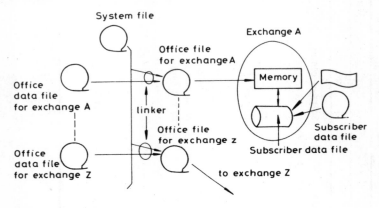

Fig. 11.6   *File generation*

11.3.2 System file

Fig. 11.7 shows the process for generating a system file. The system source file is called a MOTHER FILE, in which the programs and system data for all D-10 family systems are recorded in assembly language form. Various kinds of system file, such as for local exchange system, trunk exchange system, trunk/local exchange system etc., are generated from the MOTHER FILE. The system file generated is finally linked with the office data file and converted to the office file.

11.3.3 Office data file

Fig. 11.8 shows the office data generating process. The specific arrangements for each office are written onto special forms from which they are punched on cards and recorded in a magnetic tape called *office data source file*. Then, the office data source file is converted into the office data file by the *office data generator program*. This program converts the original office data forms into the actual office data, as explained in the previous Section. Then, the office data file is linked with the system file and supplied to the exchange site as the office file. Afterwards, the office data will be changed from time to time as the exchange grows or some office conditions change.

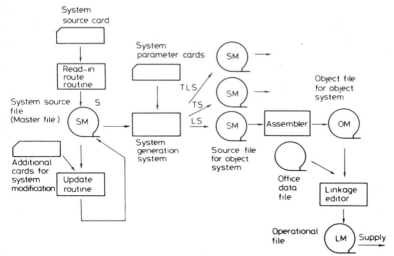

Fig. 11.7   *System file generation*

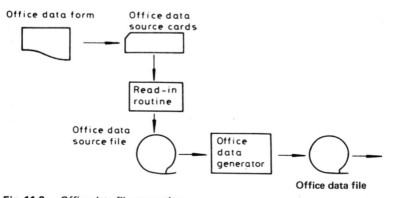

Fig. 11.8   *Office data file generation*

There are two ways of updating office data.

(i) *Updating at the exchange site:* Maintenance engineers at the exchange site can change the office data by special commands, within the limits of minor change in the office conditions or minor expansion usually irrelevant to the hardware expansion. Several kinds of commands are provided with the online program for this purpose.

(ii) *Updating at the software centre:* Fig. 11.9 shows the flow for updating the office data file at the software centre, which usually accompanies a hardware expansion. Note that the updating must be started, not from the 'original' office data file but from the one that is regenerated from the operational file at the exchange site because some of the office data may possible have been changed at the exchange site. Finally, the 'differential' office data are supplied to the exchange site in the form of paper tape.

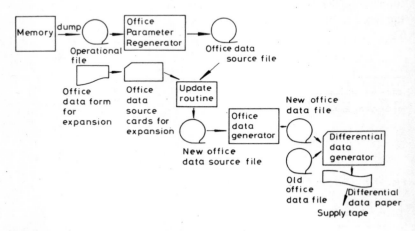

Fig. 11.9 *Office data updating flow*

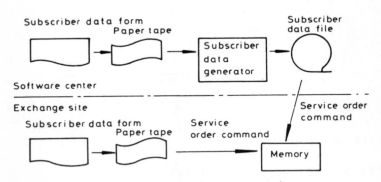

Fig. 11.10 *Subscriber data generation flow*

11.3.4 Subscriber data file

Daily work at the exchange site involves installing new subscribers and changing the number or classes of service for installed subscribers.

Accordingly, the subscriber data is generally left to the control of each exchange site for easy management. For this purpose, some convenient management tools called the service order command (as described in Chapter 9) are provided within the online program. However, it is a tool suited for a small scale of installation or changes daily required at exchange site. In the case where a bulk of subscriber data is required for installation or changes, a new subscriber data file is generated by the subscriber data generator at the software centre for saving time and supplied to the exchange site in the form of magnetic tape, as shown in the Fig. 11.10.

Chapter 12

The software centre and its support programs

12.1 The need for a software centre

The previous Chapter has outlined some of the various types of support programs required to create and manage the office file required for loading into an electronic switching system. These support programs must run on a data processing centre, commonly called the software centre. The software centre may consist of a standard general purpose computer, or it may be based on an extended version of the ESS processor itself. In the case of D-10 the latter approach has been taken since it is guaranteed that this hardware will be available and maintained for the life of the D-10 system, whereas the product life of a commercial data processing system is generally considerably shorter than that of a switching system. The use of a commercial system therefore carries the risk of lack of maintenance at some time in the future, or else software modification when the machine is changed.

A software centre may be regarded as a 'factory' which provides the functions of:

(a) program production (development)
(b) program modification and extension (maintenance)
(c) office data production (for new exchanges)
(d) office data modification and additions (for growth)
(e) production of copies of the system file (mass production).

Since a software centre is nothing more than a special purpose data processing centre, an operating system is required to control the flow of work through the centre.

12.2 Software centre operating systems

12.2.1 Objectives of the operating system

The generation of a system file involves a sequence of a large number of processes such as converting assembly instructions to machine code, editing of various data files, merging various files, and so on. An operating system is designed to automate this flow of work through the system. Each user of the system defines the process required by the use of a *job control language* (JCL) which defines the process to be performed, what resources are required, and what to do in the event of a failure at some stage of the process.

A second aim of an operating system is to improve the efficiency of the use of the data processing system by multiprogramming. This implies that many jobs may be processed simultaneously and any processor idle time in the process of a particular job (caused by input/ output limitation) is assigned to other jobs.

The third aim of an operating system is to provide a set of standard tools to the user. These main tools include

(i) *Language processors* which convert one form of program to another. These include assemblers, macro convertors, and various high level language compilers.

(ii) *Input/output control functions* to control the flow of information between the various devices attached to the data processor.

(iii) *Common utilities* such as text editors, linking programs, data generators, and so on.

The main components of the software centre operating system are shown in Fig. 12.1. They are divided into control programs and processing programs.

Control programs correspond to the execution control program and fault recovery programs of the online system. They include

(*a*) *system control program* which has the function of loading the operating system into the main memory and then starting it. It also is responsible for administering the hardware configuration and providing communication between operator and the operating system. Finally, it is responsible for the collection of operational statistics.

(*b*) *job control program* which supervises the flow of jobs through the system by interpreting the instructions on the job control cards. This program is also responsible for providing the multiprocessing capability.

(*c*) *task control program* which handles the actual tasks involved in a job; it is responsible for allocation of memory space and loading the tasks.

(*d*) *data control program* provides the standard mean of input/output of data from the various peripheral devices.

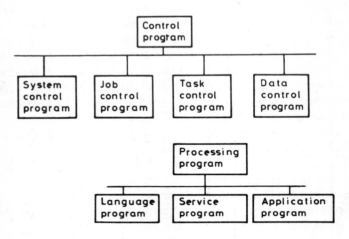

Fig. 12.1   *Operating system organisation*

Processing programs are the program groups used to actually perform the required jobs. They are discussed in detail in the next Section and include

(i) *language processors* to convert assembly code to machine code modules, to expand various types of macro statements to assembly code and to compile high level language statements to assembly code.

(ii) *linkage editor* takes a number of individual modules and links them together to form a single machine executable code module.

(iii) *office data generator/regenerator* which takes office and subscriber data as defined by the engineers and office administrators and converts this into the data format required for the system and office file. It also provides the reverse function of converting a copy of the office or subscriber data obtained from an operational office and regenerating the input that could have generated this. This function is required during an expansion or rearrangement of an office.

(iv) *patch edit control system* for administration of minor modifications of operational systems.

(v) *system generator* for supervision of MOTHER FILE.

The latter two programs are discussed in the next Chapter.

Assembly language			Machine language (hexadecimal expression)	Meanings
C 1 Name field (2 to 11)	Operation field (12 to 18)	Operand field (19 to 30)		
	T	,3/28,3	0D03031C	What are the contents of 3 bits from 28th bit of register #3?
	JNZ	/CE010	42E00003	Jump to CE010 (3 words ahead) if the result of the above is ≠0.
	T	,3/27,1	0D03011B	Is 27th bit of register #3 = 0 or ≠0?
	JNZ	/CE080	42E0000F	Jump to CE080 (15 words ahead) if the result of the above is ≠0.
CE010	L	4,3/21,2	11430215	Bring only 2 bits from 21st bit of register #3 to register #4.
	ST	4/BUFFER	A1408105	Store the contents of register #4 in the BUFFER.

Fig. 12.2 *Correspondence between Assembly language and Machine language (example)*
Note: The address of BUFFER shall be 261 words ahead from the head address of the program.

12.3 Assembler

The assembler used for D-10 follows conventional lines. The basic function takes assembly code instructions punched on cards in mnemonic form with fields for label, operation code and parameters and converts

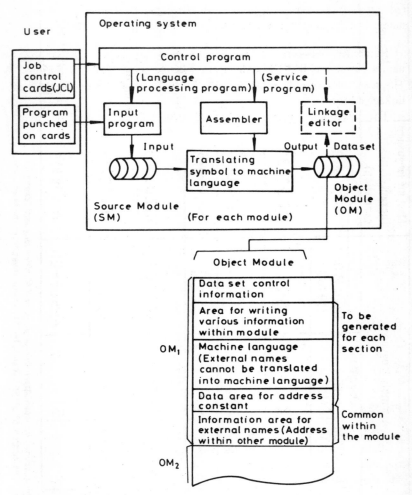

Fig. 12.3   *Assembler outline*

it into machine code modules (called object modules). A typical example of the assembly code is shown in Fig. 12.2. The source and object modules are maintained on magnetic tape rather than cards. Once a source file is on tape it may be edited by a source update routine. The structure of the assembler is shown in Fig. 12.3 and provides the function

(*a*) *grammar check* for conformity to prescribed format, duplicate definition of internal names, and so on
(*b*) *symbol conversion* which takes the mnemonic codes, symbolic names and parameters and produces relocatable machine code.

Reference between modules is performed by means of symbolic names defined as EXTERNAL in one module and ENTRY in another. The assembler produces the information required for later use by the linkage editor.

The assembler contains a standard MACRO function as shown in Fig. 12.4.

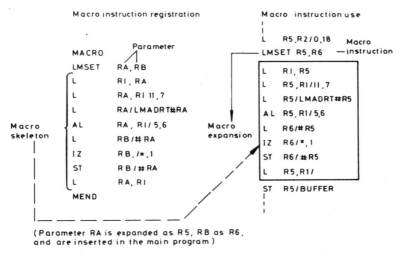

(Parameter RA is expanded as R5, RB as R6, and are inserted in the main program)

Fig. 12.4   *Macro instruction*

Data description: One of the characteristics of an ESS program is the vast amount of data used. Typically a large local switching system file may contain over 1,000K words of which 80% is data. Therefore essential requirements for the assembler are to provide ease of handling of data, prevention of errors in the use of data, and ease of addition or modification of data.

As has been seen in the program description, there is extensive use of packing whereby a number of data items are stored in one word, as can be seen, for instance, in Fig. 12.5. The machine code is provided with a number of features to process partial word operations. To deal with this situation, field definition capability is provided within the assembly language. The actual code is then written in terms of the field names, so that a modification of the data layout requires only a change of the definition statements.

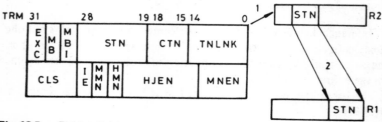

Fig. 12.5   *Field definition*
Note
*1   Here, the TRM head address is stored in R6.
*2   Field specification acts as address modifier for arithmetic instruction between memory and register. That is, in this example, since subfield STN is at address 0 of field TRM, it is converted to 'L R2/0#R6'.
*3   For arithmetic instruction between the registers, field specification acts as digit modifier. That is, in the above example, it is converted to 'L R1, R2/19, 10'.

12.4 Linkage editor

The many object code modules of instructions and data have to be linked together to produce a *load module*. The linkage editor which performs this function is shown in Fig. 12.6. It provides two main functions

(i) *External name processing* which finds the links between modules which have been specified by symbolic addresses and converts them to absolute addresses
(ii) *Address constant processing* which converts symbolic addresses stored in the data sections into absolute addresses.

12.5 Office data generator

The previous Chapter explains how the office data for a particular office is produced separately. This data is controlled by the *office data generator* (DGN) program which takes the data input expressed in a simple (humanoriented) format and converts it into an object module. The main aims of the DGN program are to be labour-saving and to ensure accuracy. Typically an office with 10,000 terminations requires about 20K words of office data. However the specification of this data requires only about 10% of this data to be input. The remaining expansion and linkage data is created by the DGN program.

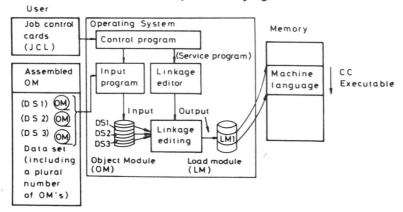

Fig. 12.6   *Linkage editor outline*

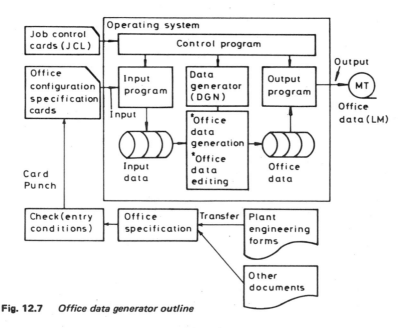

Fig. 12.7   *Office data generator outline*

The DGN processing is outlined in Fig. 12.7. The sequence of operation is as follows

(i) *Plant engineering:* When the installation design for a particular office is finalised, the plant engineering forms become the source data for the office data. This data includes the amount of equipment installed, network wiring, arrangement of trunks, translation tables, and so on.

(ii) *Office configuration specification and card generation:* The office configuration specification sheets are filled in based on the data obtained from the plant engineering form. The information used is shown in Table 12.1 and is punched onto cards.

Table 12.1   *Office configuration specification list (LS + CTX)*

Type of office specification	Contents
Common equipment	Equipment mounting and connection states
Network	Equipment mounting and accommodation states Junctor subgroup connection states
Trunks	Equipment mounting and accommodation states Use of TSG in one trunk package Use of TB
Number translation and routing	Originating/terminating number translator expansion Decision on the number of digits of outgoing/incoming lines Information on trunk class Route bypass conditions Local office numbers use
CTX	Equipment connection and accommodation states Services for tenants
Miscellaneous data	

(iii) *Office data generation:* The office specification cards plus control cards specifying the type of office, allowances for growth, memory allocation, and so on, are input to the DGN program which checks the consistency of the input data and produces an *office data load module*.

(iv) *Office file generation:* The office file consists of an office data load module and a system program module and these must be linked by the linkage editor to produce the office file for a particular office.

Chapter 13

Program standardisation and management

13.1 Need for standardisation

The great virtue of stored program controlled switching systems compared with electromechanical systems is the separation of the spc system into hardware and software components with a well defined interface specification. This interface consists primarily of speech path control orders. As long as these specifications are followed, either the hardware or software may be developed and improved independently. Hardware engineers may devote themselves to improvements in performance and economy without concerning themselves about the detailed functions of switching systems and software engineers can concern themselves with upgrading services and adding new functions. In addition, hardware specifications are fixed early and are stable since features and enhancements are provided by software. This enables economies in the cost of manufacturing facilities, drawings, training, and so on.

As the majority of improvements are in the software it is more easy to keep each system in the field up-to-date with the latest release. In the electromechanical systems it is generally uneconomic to make all engineering changes on all systems so there exists a wide variety of systems in the field with the attendant difficulties of documentation and training.

However, with software the 'ease of modification' introduces its own problems. Anybody can readily change programs or service provided for customers, without special manufacturing facilities, such as tools, parts and wires. If no limitation is imposed on program modification, this can result in many variations of those programs. Existence of such program variations tends to make it difficult to add functions to a system, or impairs, by itself, that ease of expanding functions which is the original purpose of using a program-controlled switching system.

Hardware specifications are supported by a vast number of manufacturing drawings maintained in each manufacturing company and by factory facilities resulting from a high level of investment. Modification of such specifications necessitates a change in a large number of those drawings and facilities and therefore the modification process becomes troublesome. In other words, such manufacturing drawings and facilities act as inertia and result in establishment of a rigid management organisation to control it.

On the other hand, software does not have such an inertia and it is therefore necessary to organise a special management system to control the modifications required.

Switching systems are functionally grouped into local, trunk, local and trunk combined with or without special services and CENTREX. In addition, mobile telephone switches and video switches are now under development. The size and organisation of a switch differs from one office to another. In addition there will be continuing improvements in hardware which take advantage of advances in hardware technology and components.

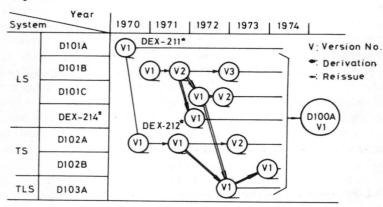

Note: Asterisk means a name at development

Fig. 13.1   *Progress of D-10 switching program practical use*

Thus, it is anticipated that electronic switching systems will be applied to wider fields year by year and hardware will be improved depending on advances in its components. These changes will be accompanied by derivative development of a lot of programs. This trend is apparent as seen from the development in the early days of D-10 programs as is shown in Fig. 13.1. This trend was expected to continue in the future.

The design of programs for individual offices under such diverse conditions can lead to a deadlock in the design and management processes, and apparently spoil software expansibility.

As described in the previous Chapter, software generalisation and standardisation to cater for conditions which change between offices within an office type are a basic problem in SPC systems. Technically, software must also be generalised to cater for changes in office type so as to avoid the maintenance of a large number of different programs.

The method which is adopted in D-10 is to strictly divide the program into common and individual programs, according to their fields of application, and manage them in uniform manner, since most programs can be used in common, although various types of switching stage and hardware are involved. This method is called *program standardisation*.

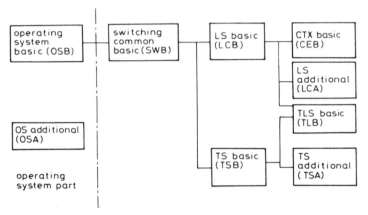

Fig. 13.2   *Function modules hierarchy*

13.2 Standardisation technique

MOTHER FILE

The standardisation technique adopted in D-10 is based on the concept of what is called a MOTHER FILE. This MOTHER FILE consists of 'switching functional blocks' which form a hierarchy as shown in Fig. 13.2. Each functional block contains 'elementary switching functional modules' (called 'program units' or simply 'units') which can be united in a variety of combinations to meet the switching system requirements, depending on switching functions and the class of office. Each unit is designed to be functionally self-contained, conceptually easily understandable and to have a small and simple interface with the other units.

The MOTHER FILE contains about 470 program units and the average size of a unit is about 740 words. Most of the units (approximately 75%) are smaller than the average. These units form source modules and are the minimum entities of maintenance in MOTHER FILE. The MOTHER FILE is maintained by means of unit registration, unit deletion, unit change, and so on. For example, when a new switching function must be introduced into the switching system, new units corresponding to the function are added to MOTHER FILE (unit registration).

The system program is produced from the MOTHER FILE through the procedure in which individual units are selected from the MOTHER FILE and combined together. This procedure is called 'system generation' (SG).

The functions of a particular class of switching system are characterised by the several parameters (called 'system parameters'). These parameters are also used in the system generation process to select and combine units. An example of the system parameters is shown in Table 13.1.

Table 13.1   *System parameter example*

Parameters	Set value	Contents
&STG	LS, TS, TLS	Classification switching stage
&CS	0, 1	Existence of common channel signal function
&R1	0, 1	Existence of remote-control function
&TV	0, 1	Existence of video switching function

According to the system parameters, system generation is carried out by the following procedure:

(i) Functional block selection
(ii) Unit selection
(iii) Grouping of these selected units into segments according to the type of memory they require
(iv) Linking of these segments and allocating of absolute memory addresses to them.

(v) Detailed program modifications by the conditional assemble facilities.

The above SG procedure is shown in Fig. 13.3.

Thus, the following information is required for the SG procedure:

(*a*) Selection conditions for each functional block
(*b*) Selection conditions for each unit
(*c*) Linking conditions for each segment
(*d*) Memory allocation for each switching system.

The above information has to be maintained as well as the MOTHER FILE.

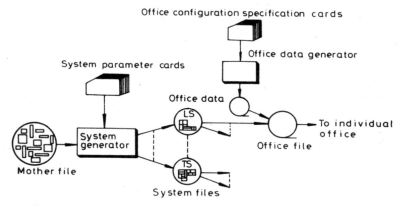

Fig. 13.3 *System generation process*

To obtain an object system with the required functions, it is necessary to explicitly describe the common relationship of programs according to function. Generally, a hierarchy diagram is used in which programs are grouped in functional modules and ranked in order of their scope of common use, as shown in Fig. 13.2.

In this Figure, the CTX module ranks below the LS (local switch) module. This means that each unit of the CTX module can be designed on the assumption that all the units in the LS module exist and that the CTX module cannot operate without the LS module. In other words, a system incorporating CTX function always provides LS function.

The features of the modules are as follows.

Operating system – Basic (OSB): This module functions as the operating system for the essential real-time processing for a switching machine. This module is also applicable to the processing other than telephone switching. It consists of units which provide the following functions:

(*a*) Execution control
(*b*) Memory control
(*c*) Timing control
(*d*) I/O equipment control
(*e*) System configuration control
(*f*) Fault-recovery processing for common equipment
(*g*) Common equipment diagnosis
(*h*) Common control for man-machine interface

Telephone switching common module – Basic (SWB): This module provides functions common to all the switching stages. It consists of I/O control program, task language interpreter, access method program to common data, and so on.

Other basic modules (LCB, CEB, TSB, TLB): These modules provide the basic functions specific to each class of office. In this system it is subdivided into four modules (LS, TS, CTX and TLS). They mainly provide call processing tasks or additional functions for individual classes of office.

Additional modules: These modules, associated with each class of office, are available for optional incorporation into object system. For example, the LS module has options to include TV telephone module and/or remote control module.

Modularisation principles

The efficiency of assembling program units, like building blocks, largely depends on the principles by which each unit is modularised. For D-10 the following principles are used:

(i) The function of one program unit should be simple, clear and explicitly definable. Function overlapping among two or more units should be avoided.

(ii) Linkages with other units should be as few and simple as possible. From the execution control point of view, a unit should have a simple structure, preferably one entry and one exit.

(iii) A unit should have an internal structure based on a series of consistent algorithms.

(iv) As a minimum object of maintenance, a unit should be of easily manageable size, preferably less than 1,000 words.

(v) Total number of units should also be of manageable magnitude, preferably less than 500 units.

A unit modularised as above is then programmed and filed to form a source module unit, which becomes a minimum object in the program file maintenance. At the same time, documents are also provided for every program unit.

Measures taken to improve modularity
It is difficult to specify evaluation criteria of unit modularity. Practically, however, functional integration and the separation of each unit are important. This is particularly difficult for the call processing program because of the high degree of multiple-processing on a time-division basis under severe requirements of reliability and economy.

(a) Functional separation
The call processing program is characterised by the use of the state-transition diagram as its structural basis. The diagram consists of stable states, where calls in them are monitored by input programs, and of transitions from one state to another, which will take place as a result of an input (e.g. lifting the telephone handset, dialling). Every transition on the diagram has a corresponding piece of program called 'task program', which carries out switching operations required for the transition. Stable states are assigned to different function modules, according to the types of call they describe. Accordingly, task programs belong to different function modules, too.

Task programs were originally numbered by a two-dimensional number such as

(Pretransition)		(Transition number)
( )	−	( )
(state number)		(to this state)

Hence, task programs belonged to their respective pretransition states, and thus to function modules to which the states belonged. Because transitions from such states as 'dialled digit reception' branch out in a tree-like form to a number of states that belong to different function modules to which post-transition states belong. In other words, task programs are more strongly characterised by post-transition states than by pretransition states. Therefore, the task program numbering scheme is changed to

(Post-transition)		(Transition number)
( )	−	( )
(state number)		(to this state)

This change is illustrated in Fig. 13.4.

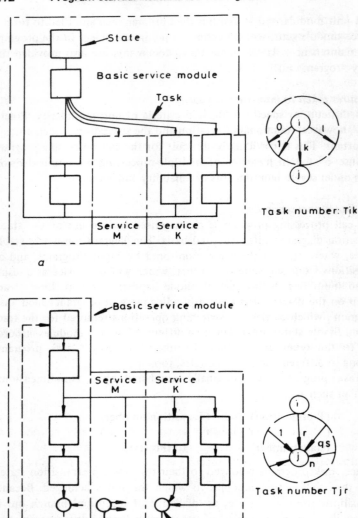

Fig. 13.4   *Task numbering scheme*
   a Numbering by prestate number
   b Numbering by poststate number

(*b*) *Use of problem-oriented interface macro*
Switching programs have an enormous amount of common data. Since they interface with speech path hardware and switching signals at many places, changes of these data have serious effects on the interface among programs. Therefore, it is necessary to use interface macros for communication with them and this macro was chosen to be problem-oriented to facilitate additions or changes of functions. Its effect is shown with an example.

In selecting an outgoing trunk and starting the incoming trunk of the called office, it is possible to distinguish trunk signals and describe the process in macro language, as follows.

SOP B0	:	S relay operation of outgoing trunk circuit
SOP B1	:	S relay operation of outgoing sender trunk circuit
DLAY STT	:	Constant timing
ZSCN	:	Check of start complete signal of the called office.

With this method, however, changes are made at scattered places within a program when a trunk's relay control sequence is changed or a signal system is added.

It is naturally more effective to use the problem-oriented macro given below and to distinguish signals and to describe a physical control method in the macro.

STK B0, B1 : (Starting and checking called office)

(*c*) *Logical expression of parameters*
The method of specifying macro parameters directly with numeric values presented some problems, namely the difficulty of value alterations and the lack of symbolic significance. For instance, the TMTS is a time-setting macro and a macro expression, such as TMTS B0, S, 10, was used conventionally for taking up 10 s of timing. To modify this to 20 s required alterations to be made at scattered places.

This can be considerably simplified if the expression TMTS B0, S, PSPD, is followed by the macro definition of PSPD = 10, because the change of this single macro definition is sufficient for altering the timing throughout the program.

That is why logical expressions are adopted throughout the system in place of the conventional expression in terms of absolute value level.

(*d*) *Common data access restriction only through authorised macros*
All data and tables, which are commonly referred to by programs, are

classified as common data and form separate program units. Office data is always classified as common data, too. In case their structure or format is changed, corrections that are necessary to meet the change would require a tedious task of finding all of their references in the whole program and correcting them one by one, if access to them were not made through some limited number of macros. Hence, to facilitate program maintenance and reduce linkage between program units, access to common data is restricted to be made only through authorised macros. By this arrangement, changes of common data can be met collectively by changing macro definitions alone and reassembling the whole program.

Further care that has been paid in defining program units include separation of programs, that are vulnerable to hardware or service specification changes, into independent program units.

Application of conditional assembly

Strict subdivision into program units, according to their exact functions would lead to a multitude of similar program units with slight differences. To cope with the situation, conditional assembly is applied to absorb minor differences and thus reduce the total number of program units in the MOTHER FILE to a manageable magnitude (less than 500, as mentioned before). Conditional assembly provides such statements as follows, so that programmers may direct the assembler in its act of assembling.

> AIF parameter = value ELSE AGOTO label;
> AGOTO label;

The first statement informs the assembler that, if the parameter value is equal to the specified value, subsequent statements should be assembled, otherwise they should be skipped until the specified label. The second statement just tells the assembler to skip assembling until the specified label. Parameter values are supplied to the assembler at the time of assembly, according to the class of office for which the present assembly is undertaken. They are given as system generation parameters. Thus, system generation parameters are used both to select program units from the MOTHER FILE and also as conditional assembly parameters at the time of assembly after the selection.

Although conditional assembly is an effective tool, it reduces clarity and understandability to a certain degree. Hence, its use is restricted to such cases as to:

(i)   Eliminate logical errors

(ii) Form linkage among selected units

(iii) Reduce memory occupancy, for example, more than 50 words per unit

(iv) Increase processing capacity, for example, more than 0·05% per use.

Fig. 13.5 illustrates an example of conditional assembly in use.

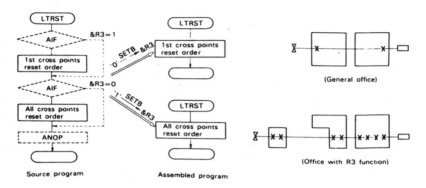

Fig. 13.5 *Application of conditional assembly*

In a standard office, the program does not reset crosspoints when a call is completed. However, when a switch-block is situated remote from the main machine it is necessary to reset the crosspoints to avoid crosstalk.

Connection data units

Linkage among program units that belong to different function modules is to be formed only through 'connection data'. They are gathered in connection data units. Conditional assembly is often used in them to tailor connection data to linkage patterns that differ from one generated program to another, according to the object office.

They are used, as shown in Fig. 13.6, and are equivalent, in a hardware sense, to cabled connectors provided to interconnect circuit boards or individual equipments.

Some connection data examples are program activation timetables, program address tables, and task decision tables.

13.3 File production and modification

To accommodate the functional modification and expansion of the D-10 system, the MOTHER FILE is updated periodically. New offices are always supplied with the newest version of the system program. The system file production is carried out at the software centre. This job is called SG job. The system generation requires the intricate procedure of SG job planning and scheduling, because the switching program size is very large and the SG process contains many steps and SG job therefore requires various centre resources. The system generator (SGN) has been developed to make the above procedure easy and precise. SGN produces the switching program from MOTHER FILE according to system parameters.

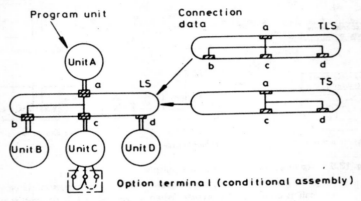

Fig. 13.6   *Connection data unit*

On the other hand, in minor function changes and bug correction, a patching scheme has been used, as this method allows immediate modification and verification of modification results. The patch is described in machine language and absolute addresses. However, the system programs, produced from the same MOTHER FILE, are different in their organisation and absolute addresses, depending on the unit selection and its conditional assembly. Therefore, the patches have to be produced on an individual switching system basis from the modification information of the MOTHER FILE. The patch area, which is the patch data storage area in a memory, and supplied patches also have to be managed on an individual system basis for latter patch production. The patch converting system (PCS) has been developed to make this patch production easy and precise. PCS automatically produces the patch data for each different switching system.

The total support system mainly composed of SGN and PCS is called the system file producing system (SFPS). The system file production process supported by SFPS is shown in Fig. 13.7.

For major function modification, first, the MOTHER FILE is updated, then the system files are produced from the MOTHER FILE by SGN according to the system parameters. After comprehensive tests on the produced program, the system program is linked with office data and then supplied to each office. On the other hand, for minor changes in function or bug correction, the modification information of the MOTHER FILE, which is written in source language, is translated into the patch data written in machine language by PCS. PCS also produces the system file containing patches called the patched load module file (PLF), which can be used for the live switching program in the switching system. These PCS outputs are supplied to each switching office in service.

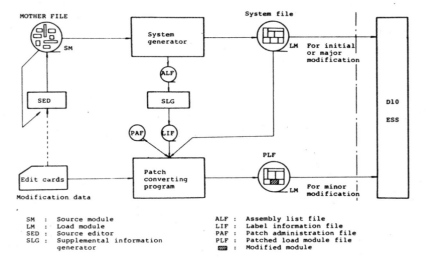

SM	:	Source module	ALF	:	Assembly list file
LM	:	Load module	LIF	:	Label information file
SED	:	Source editor	PAF	:	Patch administration file
SLG	:	Supplemental information	PLF	:	Patched load module file
		generator	▨	:	Modified module

Fig. 13.7　*System file producing system*

The input cards of PCS can be used in MOTHER FILE modification without further conversion. The necessary information for SG execution and patch production, such as attribute information on each unit and supplied patch information of each switching system, is managed by SFPS.

Thus, a unified and effective maintenance method based on the MOTHER FILE concept has been established by using SFPS.

13.3.1 Patch converting system (PCS)
PCS has two major functions. One is the address conversion function, which converts a given source statement number in MOTHER FILE

into an absolute address in system program and the other is code translation function which translates input modification data described in
assembly language into adaptive machine language for system program.

The latter function not only translates source statements but also
generates the linking instruction code which links the main program to
the patch area. The above conversion requires some conversion-aid
information, such as patch area information and label information and
so on.

The above information is contained in the label information file
(LIF) which is generated from assembly list by supplemental information generator. The patch information on individual system programs
and the patch area information are automatically registered in path
administration file (PAF), and these data are referred to at the latter
patch conversion. Address conversion and code translation examples
for the case of insertion modification are shown in Fig. 13.8.

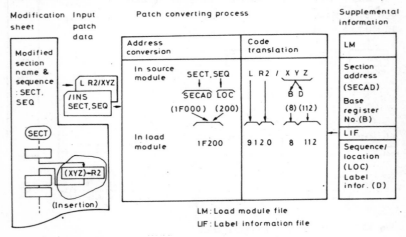

Fig. 13.8   *Example of patch control*

A live switching file is replaced with PLF by using the file updating
function contained in switching program. This procedure is available
for eliminating the error caused by inputting the patches in irregular
sequence.

13.4 Program system management

In view of the original purpose of the SPC technology for incorporating
changes in external environments, it is quite natural to expect constant

additions or modifications of switching programs. Since the system management is realised in a simple manner by the MOTHER FILE concept, it is important to determine how to deal with the MOTHER FILE on practical operations.

The following basic principles are taken in this respect:

(*a*) The system is constantly reissued every other year.
(*b*) Functions to be added or modified shall be integrated into the latest issue only. Those reflecting on immediate service may be exempted from this restriction and be added into the currently operating system on a temporary basis.
(*c*) Older issue operating in existing offices shall be replaced with the latest issue at an earliest possible time.

Under this policy, it is possible to deal with only one issue of the system for adding functions at any one time and with two or three issues for daily maintenance. Thus, it is believed that improved functions can be added in a most systematic and successful manner.

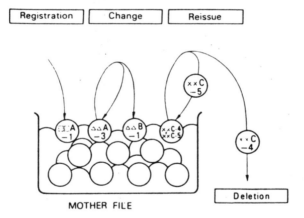

Fig. 13.9   *Management of units*

All of the additions or modifications of functions in the system issue are implemented in terms of units as the smallest management unit. As shown in Fig. 13.9, the following four fluctuating patterns of the unit exist:

(i) *Registration:* This means addition of new functions into the MOTHER FILE.
(ii) *Deletion*
(iii) *Reissue:* This means to delete and replace the old issue with a new one after reissue.

(iv) *Change:* This situation may arise when the old unit may not be replaced with a new one after change. This is the case when a new contol unit, say, for the typewriter due to type change, is added into the MOTHER FILE, and such a new unit coexists with the old control unit.

Facing the ever-changing external situations, it is essential to resort to the method of unit reissue by software in absorbing any change of hardware due to function additions, so that the expansion, in scale, of the MOTHER FILE is to be controlled.

As to the control functions of the hardware assumed to be deleted in the future, it is quite important to separately provide units to ease deletion of such functions.

13.5 Results and evaluation

The merits that were expected of the MOTHER FILE approach have been achieved in the project as follows.

(*a*) *Total program volume reduction.*
The number of program systems that need maintenance is decreased from the former 5 to one. In terms of program words, the former 1,350 kilo-words of the five program systems is decreased to approximately 280 kilo-words in the MOTHER FILE.

Furthermore, this reduction to only one standardised MOTHER FILE opened the way for the standardisation of relating support programs, such as office data generator. Thus, a significant reduction of total software needed to run and manage D-10 offices is achieved.

(*b*) *Document volume reduction*
Another merit that is worthy of note is the reduction in number of documents that are provided to describe the program system, either for specification or for explanation. Formerly, they amounted approximately to 320 kilo sheets of paper, but have been reduced to less than 1/5 or 60 kilo sheets. This reduction facilitates training as well as maintenance and management.

On the other hand, the MOTHER FILE has the disadvantages of:

(i) As a single program system, the volume grew larger. It is expected to grow further by future modifications or function additions.
(ii) Minor peculiarities or irregularities of certain offices cannot be isolated locally, but should be always dealt with in the MOTHER FILE, thus affecting the whole program system.

(iii) Working program production needs an additional procedure for system generation.

Some quantitative results

Fig. 13.10 gives some quantitative results obtained in the MOTHER FILE development. Comments on them follow.

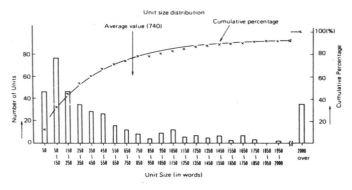

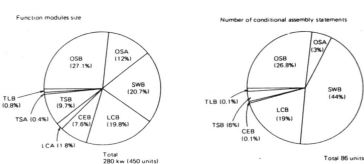

Fig. 13.10 *Quantitative results of modularisation*

(*a*) Number of program units has turned out to be 450, which is well within the original target of less than 500. Of the 450 units, 416 are program units (in its narrow sense as against data) while the rest (34) are data units.

(*b*) Average size of a unit is 740 words. Most of the units (approximately 75%) are smaller than the average. There are a number of units that exceed 2,000 words. Most of them have a large data area, such as buffer area or test data in the case of diagnosis programs. It is meaningless to separate them further.

(c) Common modules used in all the generated program files, i.e. operating system basic (OSB) and telephone switching common basic (SWB) occupy approximately 60% of the total volume of the MOTHER FILE. Again, in terms of program volume, approximately 85% of program units used in toll switching are used also in local switching. These large percentages prove one aspect of the effectiveness of the MOTHER FILE approach.

(d) The fact that units which employ conditional assembly occupy only 20% of the total units indicates the degree of modularity achieved by the program units. In other words, 80% of them are well modularised in the sense that they need no adjustments as to eliminating logical errors, forming linkage with other units and so on, as discussed before. Of the units that employ conditional assembly, more than 70% belong to common function modules, such as OSB and SWB, because conditional assembly is mostly used in connection data units to form linkage among units selected for the production of an object office. Connection data units belong to common function modules, either OSE or SEB.

Examples of state-transition diagrams

The state-transition diagram pictorially describing the switching operation which is caused by the input signal from subscriber lines or trunks, has been mentioned in the Chapters 2 and 4. This diagram not only has the advantage of the fact that the switching function specifications can be described intelligibly and accurately, but it also has a design advantage of call processing program. It is probably one of the most noteworthy features of electronic switching technology in Japan.

Examples of the local switching service are illustrated in Figs. A.1 – Fig. A.4.*

---

* Editors note: These diagrams were produced before the development of the CCITT System Description Language and in fact provided one of the major inputs to the specification of that language.

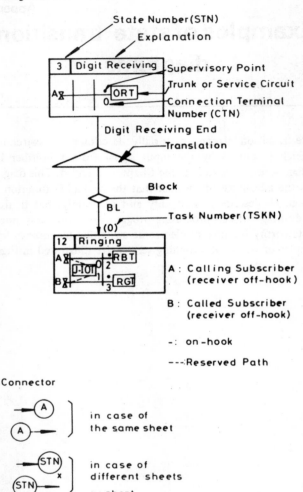

State-transition diagram

Fig. A.1 *LS basic call state-transition diagram*
Subscriber originating and release procedure

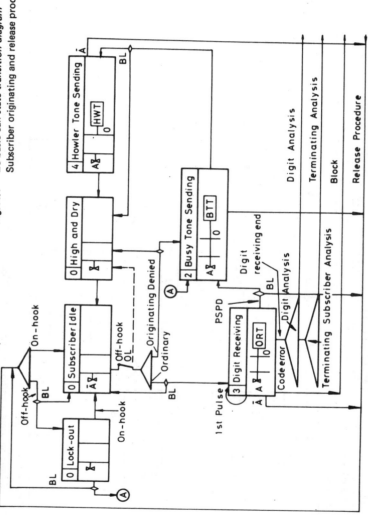

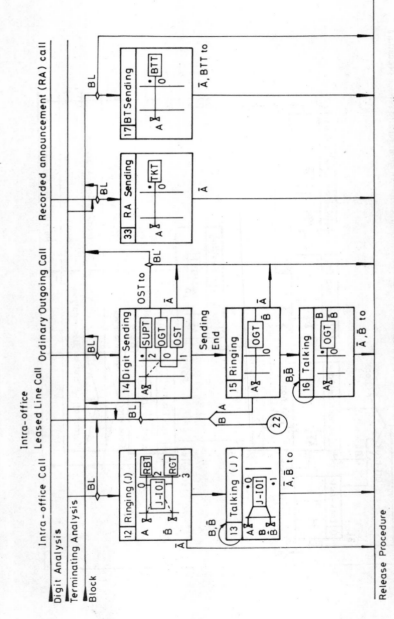

Fig. A.2 *LS basic call state-transition diagram*   Intraoffice call, ordinary outgoing call, talkie connection call

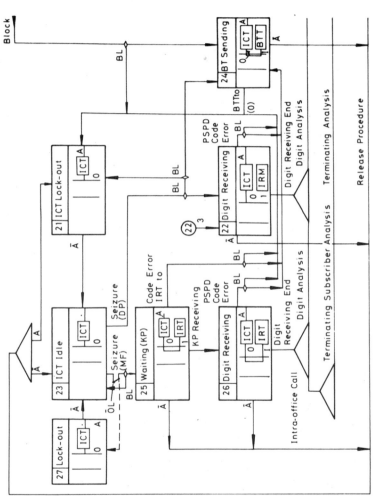

Fig. A.3   *LS basic call state-transition diagram* Ordinary incoming call, ICT release procedure

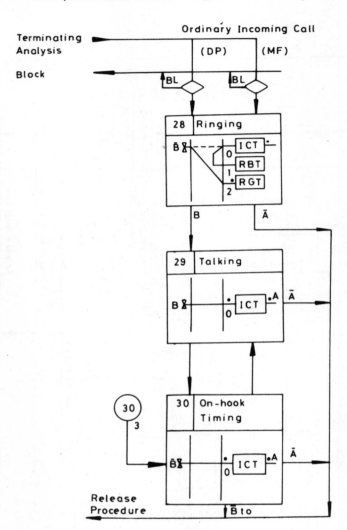

Fig. A.4   *LS basic call state-transition diagram*
Ordinary incoming call

Abbreviations

OL	overload
RC	recall signal
t.o.	time over
PSPD	permanent signal and partial dial
MB	make busy
KP	key pulse
FCG	false cross and ground
DP	decadic pulse
MF	multifrequency code
CDT	continuous dial tone
ORT	originating register trunk
BTT	busy tone trunk
HWT	howler trunk
RBT	ring back tone trunk
J-IOT	junctor-intraoffice trunk
TKT	talkie trunk
TMR	timing register
SUPT	supervisory trunk
OGT	outgoing trunk
ICT	incoming trunk
OST	outgoing sender trunk
IRT	incoming register trunk
IRM	incoming register memory
OGT-HD	outgoing holding trunk
ICT-DL	delayed toll incoming trunk
RGT	ringing tone trunk

Index